Country Li

THE NEW POACHER

In his preface to the original *Poacher's Handbook* Ian Niall wrote: 'There is no better way of studying an art than by examining the technique of the masters, and the student will find in this modest work portraits of the men whose art has been recognised by authority; men who have devoted their lives to the subject, suffered severe penalties in the dogged pursuit of their calling—fines up to five pounds and many days in prison.

'Poaching is said to be a dying art, but I do not believe this. No great art dies. Congenital poachers will father poachers. It is an old thing. Hunting is in the blood. So long as there is a warren to shelter a rabbit, a holly bush in which a bird roosts, and a hollow or a hill for a hare, there will be a man or a boy who will put his natural cunning to stalking the hare, hunting the wild thing and outwitting both the quarry and the representative of authority.'

This is a book about poaching in the old traditional style, the craft of men who knew and loved the countryside and invoked unorthodox skills rather than the crude use of modern science to catch their game, which they took sparingly, as they needed it. The lessons of the masters Ian Niall follows are lessons in the lore of nature, and this is a book for everyone who loves the countryside.

THE NEW POACHER'S HANDBOOK

FOR THE MAN WITH THE HARE-POCKET
AND THE BOY WITH THE SNARE

Ian Niall

Illustrated by Sylvanus Marston

THE BOYDELL PRESS

First published 1960
First published in COUNTRY LIBRARY 1984
by The Boydell Press
an imprint of Boydell and Brewer Ltd
PO Box 9, Woodbridge, Suffolk, IP12 3DF

ISBN 0 85115 232 5

Printed in Great Britain by
St Edmundsbury Press, Bury St Edmunds, Suffolk

DEDICATED TO SUCH CHARACTERS AS

FRANCIE McGINN
BUTCHER MURPHY
SNIB, BLACK BILL
AND LITTLE HUGH

AND TO THE MEMORY
OF MY FATHER

CONTENTS

Notes to the Revised Edition

Water has passed under the bridge since the original edition of *The Poacher's Handbook* was written, water and a salmon or two. Things, people and creatures natural to the countryside have come and gone. Even a decade ago there were more men about who remembered the squire and who recalled the word 'transported' being used. The squire was a rare bird when the book was first conceived and there were those who talked of the 'vanishing art' of the ne'er-do-well. One must admit, rather sadly, that the old poacher has become a rarity. He belonged to the old estates and nearly all the fine estates have been broken up. Poachers there are, however, in the tradition. Now and again one is run to earth by a television interviewer and proves to be both garrulous and amusing, but the poachers of my youth were not garrulous. Country rascals, they may have been, under-privileged, the social reformer might call them, but resourceful men, and their sons and grandsons have stood more than once to defend the country that nurtured them. Many hard words were addressed to me for daring to produce a handbook on poaching, but I made no apology for it when it appeared, and I make none now, repeating my original preface which, I trust, will offend none but those whose liver is sadly out of order:

There is no better way of studying an art than by examining the technique of the masters, and the student will find in this modest work portraits of the men whose art has been recognised by authority; men who have devoted their lives to the subject, suffered severe penalties in the dogged pursuit of their calling – fines up to five pounds and many days in prison.

Poaching is said to be a dying art, but I do not believe this. No great art dies. Congenital poachers will father poachers. It is an old thing. Hunting is in the blood. So long as there is a warren to shelter a rabbit, a holly bush in which a bird roosts, and a hollow or a hill for a hare, there will be a man or a boy who will put his natural cunning to stalking the hare, hunting the wild thing and out-witting both the quarry and the representative of authority.

Two thoughts come to mind as I consider these words. The rabbit has declined and come near to extermination, and we have a new generation of wilder and desperate poachers, men without scruple or conscience. Let me say that I do not subscribe to the preservation of the rabbit under any circumstances and I have no time for the slaughterer of deer, or the man who is using the spring gun and frogman's gear to rob the salmon pool. If I have a decided sympathy for the ghost of the old poacher who still manages to touch the heart of many a just and upright magistrate when he comes to the dock, I have none for the gang, none for any save the individualist, the man whose skill and guile earned him his due reward and who was indeed often tolerated by the owner of land to an extent that infuriated his underlings. A word for the courage of the poachers in the days of pitched battles might be construed as indicating one's preference for anarchy, but I am not a man of violence. Anything can be taken by storm, a pheasant or a citadel, and I would speak only of art and artifice. I can only add that these words are no apology for resurrecting a work that lays out a pattern of lawlessness. One doesn't make a poacher. He is born. Most readers, I think, will expect no apology and I trust that what I say will place none of them a pace beyond the line of rectitude, nor take any of them away from a comfortable armchair and fire.

Harvest of Idleness

WHAT I have to say is truly the harvest of idleness and yet, in its way, it is the fruit of the old tree of knowledge. I was born a day-dreamer and I confess it without shame. From my earliest days I listened to the cackle of the grouse on the moss-hags and the wing-flapping of arrogant, crowing pheasants. My mind so often ran away with the breeze swaying the cotton grass and sending the thistledown soaring into the soft sky of summer. I have seen the ruffled throat of the challenging black-cock and heard the beating of their pinions as they fought below a gnarled thorn. The hunter being strong in me (psychologists, I believe, class hunters as uncomplicated men), I longed to bring home my own dinner, to have my hands on the slender stock of an old hammer gun and put up my protesting moor-cock. The moor-cock speeds into the background of brown peat and skims the contours of the heather-covered ground and is no easy target. The hare ran to make me think of hunting him and bringing him head over heels to a standstill. The woodcock's turns and twists through a hazel copse were to train my eye and teach me to control my impulses, and the trout that swung at anchor in the amber water of the burn was there to inspire me to ways of bringing him to my breakfast plate. I have come now, less strong in wind and limb, perhaps, to plan the undoing of my fish with a floating fly, but what of that? Have I more skill or more conceit of myself? If this be taken as a confession of misspent years, I admit at once that could I walk the same path again I would do so. I dearly wish I could, for no youngster of today could have a happier or healthier up-bringing than to live in the rolling country of my child-hood and to learn the minutiae of natural life. Let the amoeba be studied where the microscope is found, the place to watch a hunting weasel is where it hunts.

There never were many real poachers, men with a close affinity with nature, who poached for the love of it first and financial necessity second. Here and there one noted them, gnarled as the scrub oak, knowing as the crow, elusive as the marsh bird slipping through a reed bed. It might seem a paradox if I use the term honest poacher, but better men than I am will admit to having known honest rogues and loved them for their roguery. I go back through my crowd-ing years to days when I had time to listen to the song of the yellow-hammer, to days when the corncrake rasped in the meadow grass and hoeing boys crawled slowly on bag-wrapped knees along the rows of swedes. For some reason it seems to me that the tang of the swede field was stronger then and the cry of the nightjar, hawking moths at dusk, was much commoner than it is now. There were more pheasants to go clattering out of woods, more hares to run through the secret paths among the upland mountain ash trees, more partridges dust-bathing in the lea of little knolls, and more tall trees to mark the skyline.

I was not entered to poaching. The cloak of respectability was regularly placed about my small shoulders, but I was brought up in what might be described as a poaching countryside. It was remote in the sense that no one from outside found any reason to intrude, except, of course, the seasonal shooting parties. The sea-trout crowded the pools below the bridge, the salmon ascended as handsome fish will, the grouse picked grit on the rough moorland road where the centre strip was for ever faintly tinged with green, partridges called until evening grew old and honey-suckle scents drenched the air. There was time to stand and stare. Two sorts of beauty I found in my world, the beauty of the natural scene and the beauty of old, Damascus-barrelled guns with walnut stocks of graceful shape. There was, too, a certain kind of beauty in the tools of the rabbit-trapper and the mole-catcher, a beauty of utilitarian things that a countryman will understand. I was never a professional poacher. I applied myself diligently to the business and sold some of the proceeds, but only to buy cartridges, and they were cheap enough, no more than half a crown and of foreign make, which meant that be-times one must peer through a screen of smoke after being rocked by a fierce recoil, or stand wondering how far the shot had gone, so erratic were the loads.

Long ago I put all these things behind me, but not with-out a nostalgia which has lasted all my life and carries me often to the kitchen of my grandfather's house and snatches of half-remembered talk in the forenight while the moon rose and pines in the garden swayed and sighed – the irresponsible, impressionable years when a youngster's blood is first stirred.

A man named Jeck was my first teacher. If he is still alive, which I sadly doubt now, he must be a great deal less nimble than when I was his pupil at five years of age. Jeck worked for us to the annoyance of neighbours who had game on their land. He was unreliable as a worker. One day he would be at the plough, plodding the hill with the gulls behind him and the next he would be missing. From our biggest hill, a hog's back topped by a fir planting (long since cut down, alas), most of the countryside could be seen. Jeck could see the river; the little woods that clogged the hollows, ran along lesser hills and stretched back into the moss. Sometimes I stumbled and staggered up to the plough with his tea can and buttered scones and he would crouch on his heels, take a mouthful of tea, a bite of scone and look dreamily at the landscape to the west.

'Johnnie boy,' he would say, 'see yonder? It's the greatest place for an old cock pheasant. I seen the day when I could walk quiet along yon hedgeside, slip through the fence an' let fly.'

And the next day Jeck would be missing. Perhaps I would hear that he had seen such a day again, but I was a very small boy, and small boys are rarely the recipients of confidences that might put a man in prison.

Before the schoolmaster, who needed a strap to inculcate knowledge, had conveyed the sequence of the alphabet to my brain, Jeck had given me the way of straightening snare wire, forming the pear-shaped noose, yes, and the vital intelligence of the setting height and the place in which to set. I put down my first snare under Jeck's supervision. It was on a stubble slope where a hare was running at night. When the alarm woke the household for the five o'clock milking, long before the grey streak of early winter dawn and the first cock-crow from the locked henhouse, I was out of bed. The frost bit my toes. I could not wait to put on stockings and lace my little boots. I had to go barefoot and half-dressed, as I often did in summer. I crossed the field, skirted the gloomy clumps of gorse and ducked under the squealing fence to come to the hillside. Before I saw my catch I could hear the thump of his powerful back legs as he bounded in the noose. I ran to him, clasped him in my arms, drew the pin and carried him homeward, while every wild kick lacerated my bare knees.

Many years later, returning from school in the south, I had the opportunity of fishing a stretch of salmon water owned by a neighbour, a privilege obtained for me by my aunts, who wanted to keep me out of disreputable company for as long as I could be diverted. I went with a borrowed net and gaff, borrowed flies and a rod like a binder whip. A whole afternoon I cast and re-cast my flies, and when the village school spilled its children on the road I was joined by a torn-trousered urchin. He unwound a length of twine to which he attached a clumsy hook. On the hook he fastened a piece of red flannel, snipped, perhaps, from his grandmother's petticoat, and cast hook and red bait into the water. In five minutes he had a pike on his line. It careered this way and that. The water swirled and gave up bubbles and the boy hastened to a stump, round which he looped his line. I watched, fascinated, while he brought the long-snouted, fierce-looking gad-fish to the bank, and then I wound up my reel, put the delicate cast back in the pouch and went home. Someone had told me when I was quite small that the way to catch a salmon was to put a prawn on a hook, use salmon roe, draw a net, or hook him out of the water at the salmon-leap, and the way to catch a pike was to use red flannel; bait a hook with a live frog, or even a mouse.

Put the conventional behind you. Put your hand in the horny palm of Francie McGinn and come to the stable to learn the knots for net-making. Look now and then at the silvery light of the moon on the cobwebbed skylight and know that this is a night for staying at home, for the moon is too full and the ground too hard and the night too still. Talk small and listen to a thing as old as the hills, as natural as the gentle swish of the fir branches, the raindrops spearing across a deep pool.

The ways of coming by a rabbit, a pheasant, partridge or trout are as numerous as the hairs on your mongrel dog. You must learn the use of a gate net, a long net, snare, ferret, purse net and many another device from a whistle to a kite. You must learn to walk softly and listen long, when to run and when to stand still; the thing to do in the black hat of night and the way to read the flushed magpie and the chatter of the jay. A pigeon in flight never crosses directly over a man in open ground. When a far-away pigeon deviates in the line of flight you must learn to watch for the subsequent movement of sheep from the hedge to the corner of the field and the horse's pricked ears. It is wrong to go hastily away like the startled partridge rising among your feet. Close at hand is the hawthorn hedge and the shadows that swallow you from the bright light of day.

In the old stable of my childhood you will hear every way of finding game and every trick in taking fish. Legends there are, too, ways that are not practised but only talked about, because they are cruel or outlandish.

Francie McGinn and I will take you across the moss where the grey hen is feeding. We will not walk with the bullock-stagger of a shooting party with beaters and luncheon baskets. For a long time we will stand in the shelter of the drystone wall, close by the nodding gorse, watching the sheep out of sight over the heather slope. When they are gone you and I will walk slowly with Francie. Watch him. He is like that old drawing of the disreputable character with the gun. Not quite the sporting gentleman, because he does not need a beater to show him where the birds sit. He has taken an interest in birds and the moor. He did not step from a panelled dining-hall to a gun-room after port last night. We will move across the peat diggings and the waterholes. The birds will rise and whirr away. Francie will thrust his gun at them and one will fall. The brown bog hare will flatten his ears and race over a rise and three snipe skim and arc out of sight. When we are back in the cover of the willow clump, men with glasses will scan the moss for us; watching the sheep for frightened movement, listening for the betraying cry of the cursed curlew.

It is not a new thing. It is old, old like the scent of peat smoke from the lonely cottage; the cairn on the hill, the never-failing flight of the wild geese in October. Kindred spirits have studied these things from the day that man first built his march walls and conserved the wild life for himself. The net is no new device, the yelp of the fox no new sound and the little brown bird rose in the clearings long ago when the fowler came after it by stealth. There is an

[7]

old look in the eye of the ragged barnyard cockerel, a strange wisdom in the crow, and the same timelessness and natural movement in the way of a tall-legged hare passing through a hill of gorse or a bog of round rushes. These things were there when man began to learn his cunning, the way of the hunter.

Bewitched Hares

TAKE the hare, take it with a net or a snare, with a sleek and speedy whippet or a crafty lurcher. It is no foolish creature to fall into the hands of man, or the jaws of a dog, without teaching its pursuer that the law of the jungle is an old and sound law, no matter how the reformers rant to the contrary and talk of barbarity. The hare, it is said, has a blind spot right in front of its head. It runs watching for the enemy in the rear, as a fleet-footed creature will. In consequence of this it sometimes comes across a ploughed field headlong into danger without being aware that its life may be forfeit. It has its moments of madness, and one, at least, has been seen to challenge and fight a tomcat, prancing on its back legs in the manner of mad hares in March. It also lends itself to the magic ways of witches. For this reason, perhaps, the squeals of a hare have a particular horror for some old country people. Shoot your hare at the witching hour and what old village crone may breathe her last? Look at the great luminous eyes of a hare caught in the light of a lantern and wonder about witchcraft if you like.

The hare runs, and invites the chase, I suppose, whether

it be by the gipsy's lurcher, the miner's whippet or the rich man's coursing dog. Let those who would beat the flat fields and drive the terrified hare into a narrowing path have their sport. My hare runs or sits and observes the wonderful light of the rising sun for a better purpose and worthier end. Although I have no great taste for hare soup and like only the flesh of a leveret fried, I have a liking for the hare and the sport of netting or stalking one.

The hare runs the grass hill and sleeps in a fold of the ground in a bed as snug, as sheltered, as that of the little field-mouse. Here a clump of hay-brown grass stands alone and conspicuous, but you can see through it. You can see the contour of the ground with its ridges of a past season's ploughing where the vetch and yarrow grow. The grass tops sway a little in the earth-close breeze and are still again. Summer has gone and no grasshopper sings. Right in the middle of the clump of grass lies the hare. His haunches are raised and his ears smooth on his neck. He is soft brown, darker brown, matched to the grass, its seeds more silvery at the tips; matched to the ground, every beautiful hair a blend with the surroundings. He sleeps in the warmth of the October or late September noon.

The scents of the field soothe him, and the senses of the hunter are drugged by the breath of the land, the scents of decay, of dying leaves and mushroom growth, by the very beauty of the shades of feeble autumn, the little red fungus on the fragment of twig, the stubble bleaching fawn. This one is the hare of the arable fields. The one from the bogs seems taller of leg and darker. When he rears among the round rushes, pausing on the patch of hair grass to take a message from the wind, he seems a bigger animal. As he moves in through the rushes he retains that impression of stature. The hare of the mountain is certainly smaller. He is grey and has a tinge of blue. He reminds those who see him of blots of frozen snow up where the air is cold and the streams are sheathed in a covering of ice. They are all wild, the hare of the rough wet hollows, the hare of the clover hill and the hare of the cold mountain, wild like the cry of the peewit and the sad and lonely flight of the heron.

One will have his sleeping place on the southern slope of a distant hill, and another in the wood where the bracken has folded upon itself in a clearing. Their movement out of the wood or across the brow will be a thing so graceful that when you see it for the first time you will stand and stare long after they are gone. You will not often get close enough to see the hare in his form. He will be gone while you clamber the drystone wall and bring loose stones about your heels. His long back legs will take him fast across the hollow, the shadow of a wind-driven cloud, through the gap and away, running easily for the meadow and the shelter of the longer grass. When you have steadied your heartbeat and brushed the grey moss of the stones from your flanks you will walk past the spot where he sleeps from mid-morn until afternoon. It will be warm with the heat of his fur and if you come and disturb it with your fumbling hands it is likely that tomorrow he will sleep elsewhere at noon, so it is as well, perhaps, that you are blind to such things.

Yonder he runs on the skyline. See him speeding for the march fence. In the early morning he will be back across the grass field, feeding in the first gold shafts of sunlight that break above the horizon. When you walk the stubble, undulating over the ground of summer's harvest, you will look up to see him going like a bird. It is the poetry of action one sees in the bounding deer, the blood horse, yes, and, in its way, the stoat, hot after his prey. Evening, and he comes bobbing down the furrow. Now he halts to take stock of the countryside or, as you or I, admire the sunset and the far-away blue shadows that hang to the woods and make the ragged mountains look restful.

There is no need for pity. He has a strong heart and a body to carry him to the steepest hilltop. He has sensitive ears and back legs with power enough to snap the woven wire of the snare, unless the poacher uses cunning.

It might be thought that a hare or a trout has no particular place, that one belongs in a parish and the other in a river or stream, but this is wrong. A fish knows a small part of the stream and is frightened once it is driven, as the poacher drives it, out of its particular swim and the pools with which it is familiar. A hare belongs in two or three fields and where a man runs upon a hare in his youth he can be fairly sure of starting one when he has come to manhood. This strange affinity with certain places is beyond the understanding of ordinary people who yet know well the homing instinct and a particular feeling for a small part of the world they themselves claim as home. There is more to it than this, however. The breed of hares that runs a hill is hard to discourage. Tumble the hare that comes speeding over the brow in October and its place on that territory will be taken by another hare of the same hue and shade. Perhaps there is a lesson for man even in this.

Up in the rough ground, on the edge of the moorland a hare meanders through the clumps of thorn, the ferns and bracken, grazing where it will, stopping, sitting up and listening, teaching a watcher the true purpose of his leisure, teaching the hunter that he needs to move slowly and look about to see where his quarry lives and where he is to be put up time and again. Studying the way of the upland hare, or the partridge, a poacher learns much and develops an instinct for the sort of ground where game belongs. As the fisherman knows a pool that should have a fish in it the moment he sets eye upon it, so the countryman knows where his hare will spring out of the round rushes, and even which direction he will take, past the thorn, over the hump, through the gap in the drystone wall and away among the feathery grass nodding in the gentle breeze.

You may walk with your gun to catch your hare asleep in the morning when the watery sunlight is like a dying fire in the east, for hares must sleep. Down wind you walk, softly, with every sense alert. The wind blows through the thorn tree, rocking the dead thistle and shrivelled dock, taking the hot breath from your lips. The dead leaves roll through the dried stalks and at every stride you feel the bite of winter making your ears tingle, and gnawing at your cheeks. Across the sleeping field you go to halt at the dyke. When you turn it will be to see him flying for the gate, going fast into the wind like a pigeon.

All your cunning was not enough. You needed a dog, a little bit of a mongrel dog without much more than his natural intelligence and a good nose, but your mongrel would have gone round to take the scent on the wind and brought you up to your sleeping hare, even if the hare slept no longer, and lay with his ears sleeked on his shoulders waiting for the moment when you would come too near, or pass on, oblivious of his sleeping place.

The way of taking your hare must be studied under such instructors as Francie McGinn and Little Hugh and Black Bill

Respectability

IF you value the opinion of the ladies of the village you will stay respectable. Old Mrs Barret will nod her head in approval and say, 'Good steady man, is John. Not like some I know, always at the poaching and getting up before the Bench.'

You will put away from you all thought of a night with the long net and sleep snug in bed. When the wind cries round the eaves and a spattering of rain goes over the window above the well of the stairs, you will turn drowsily and listen for the clock chiming the half-hour and perhaps think that had you been less of a good steady man, like those in the churchyard, you might have been walking over a carpet of fir and pine needles, pondering the shadow in the tree.

If you care nothing for respectability and, after all, respectability is in the mouths of the old women a thing relative to the strength of the latest piece of gossip, you may find the policeman less friendly and the gamekeeper making dark threats in the public bar. Have courage.

'I got my eye on him,' he will say. 'Thinks I don't know. I'm just waitin' my time. I don't want no slip-ups. I want him an' his friends to get sent up the line.'

Under such threats I lived happily and quite safely for many a season. Have no fear of this talk. He talks that way to have an excuse for his lack of wits. He hopes you will hear and be frightened. Of course he waits his time. We all wait our time. Live and let live. He is paid to catch you and but for you he might be out of work.

In Wales they speak affectionately of the 'old poachers' being about again. 'Look, there he goes,' someone will nudge his neighbour. 'Biggest old poacher for miles around. If ever you want a hare, he's the man. He's got them counted better than the keeper!' Become a poacher and they will smile every time your name is mentioned. The tenant farmers, especially those with mean landlords, too jealous of their rights and slow to carry out repairs, will close their eyes to a hurried walk through the wood and across the meadow at dusk. The bigger farmers will be distant and perhaps hostile, and the landlord, once his keeper has pointed you out to him, will look at you with acute distaste, hoping that one of his neighbours will have you before him in the prisoner's dock at Monday's court.

'Trespassing in pursuit of game,' the clerk will say, and the magistrate will frown, purse his lips and clear his throat.

'You have done a bad thing. It is wrong indeed and there is a punishment. You deserve punishment too, for you have been caught. The law will make you understand that you must not trespass in pursuit of game. You must not be caught again or you will go to prison.'

Did you see the little man in the back row? He was grey-haired and had a coloured rag tied at his throat. He was wearing corduroy trousers and an over-large jacket. His eyes were very innocent. He sympathises and shares your indignation at the injustice of your disqualification from holding a gun licence. Why, only twelve months ago he was fined ten pounds and he had no more than two rabbits in his possession when he was caught. Of course, circumstances were different. It took luck to catch Little Hugh. He didn't net his first burrow yesterday. He looks into the tree in the dark, and he knows the roosting crow from the roosting pheasant. His was a case of hard luck, and luck is a thing no one can pop into his bag when he lifts his ferret from its box.

Little Hugh gathers mushrooms and firewood. It enables him to watch and take note. He does a bit of hedging and ditching. He can manage an isolated burrow with three nets and a ferret while he is trimming and bending the sticks of the hedge. The ferret travels in his jacket pocket, as tame as the old spinster's cat. Little Hugh can take his old gun along with his ditching tools, the sickle, the mattock, the draining shovel and the hedge-knife. If the pheasant, feeding where the old corn stack once stood, ventures a little nearer the ditch, Hugh will take one shot after he has stared idly around for ten minutes or so. He can move very fast for a man of sixty. Up out of the ditch, through the wire and over to the bird and back almost before the echo has returned from the hill.

Someone comes down the field, suspicious of Little Hugh, perhaps, but the pheasant is on the bank covered by a tangle of green weed, blackberry and uprooted cress. A shot? Surprise at finding someone standing so close shows on Little Hugh's face. Yes, he heard a shot not long ago and wondered about it too. Is the keeper on his rounds? Who could be shooting at this time of day? The old gun is lying down in the ditch, balanced on three stones close to the bank. Stand clear. Small pebbles and marshy grit come swinging up on the shovel. A dog is barking the cows home. Little Hugh adjusts his cap and feels in the farthest corner of his buttonless waistcoat's pocket. When the stump of cigarette is smouldering in his sheltering palm he calls to the departing visitor. Is it nearly tea-time?

The Peacock and the Perch

BEFORE you learn to catch a hare, let me introduce you to Little Hugh and say at once that the introduction is worth no more than my standing with this great poacher. One can know such men for a long time without being invited to share their company after game.

When Little Hugh was at school he had snare-wire in his pocket and a bit of a pied dog that waited for him at the gate until he went home at night. Poaching was in his blood. Someone taught him to cut snare pegs and the ways of getting a rabbit before he had left school. At the end of his schooldays his father got him a job in the garden of the big house, but it went wrong. At that time they kept peacocks. These magnificent birds strutted the lawns and swept through the paths that were hedged by little shrubs. The gardener's boy was fascinated. He thought it would be wonderful to have one about the cottage door at home, a thing his mother could admire as she sat in the doorway peeling potatoes and keeping her eye on the smaller children. Who has not tried to carry away beauty? The taking of the peacock became a thing upon which Little Hugh set his heart and his wits. How would you catch a peacock? Run at it, embrace it and carry it away down a broad drive and across a wide tree-dotted park with every blade of grass the same height and not a shadow of cover? Could you hide a peacock and walk home with it along five winding miles of quiet road?

One afternoon the boy put the dregs of a whisky bottle on a picking of chicken meal and laid it on the flags of the path, keeping watch from the herb plot where he made pretence of working with a hoe. The peacock came. Its beak darted at the drops of meal. In a little while the bird was stupefied and Hugh quickly tied a sugar bag on its head. For the rest of the afternoon the peacock sat in drunken contemplation under a laurel bush. Could he have some geranium cuttings? begged Little Hugh. The under-gardener considered and then gave his consent. The pea-cock left the grounds in a sack from which geranium cut-tings protruded through a conspicuous hole.

The grand bird was released in the garden of the cottage. It was ruffled and bedraggled, with no tail display. Little

Hugh hastened to inform his mother. The children clustered behind her as she stood on the step, staring at the peacock in horror. The uproar had hardly reached its peak when the head gardener descended from a gig. There was a stern look on his face. The peacock, which had been ignored by the family, had had the attention of a dog and had been chased through a hole in the hedge. It looked no better than a hen-pecked bantam. The gamekeeper, who came to know Little Hugh much better in time, rounded it up and put it back in the sack. The head gardener delivered a lecture during which he brandished a stick. Finally he bade Little Hugh farewell.

Shortly afterwards Hugh was caught on the lawn of the big house. He had a rod and line with which he had been trying to lure the giant old carp that swam soberly through the pond. The owner, as lacking in a sense of humour as his carp, thundered at Little Hugh as he bore down on him.

'I'm not after your fish,' protested the youth. 'It's nobody's fish until somebody's catched him.'

Later he came to know this to be no defence. It had served as a law in feudal times and perhaps the landlord owed his rights to it, but he sheltered under a new law and Little Hugh was fined, not for the giant carp, fussy of appetite and hard to lure, but for the tasteless perch he had managed to hook, three miserable little fishes with spiky fins.

The fine had to be paid. Hugh fell in with an old man netting a burrow and in a month he had raised the money. The way of a hare he came to know and the way of a pheasant, a partridge, and, of course, the rabbit. He got to know the kind of ferret, the kind of dog to have, and the use of the gate net, long net and whistle and kite. In more than forty years he gathered all the ways of taking game and the ways of disposing of it, too. He was encouraged by an hotel-keeper, and a fish merchant who sold rabbits and an odd brace of birds. He got to know one or two people in the town who liked, and could afford, jugged hare or roast pheasant.

'Pheasant?' he will say. 'Me eat pheasant? I never tasted one in my life. Far too fancy for me, is pheasant. No, rabbit's good enough for us."

In this he differs from some of his country neighbours who hold strange beliefs concerning rabbit, which, among other things, they say breeds with rats, being a rodent, is alive with worms, and has 'the consumption something awful'.

He is well-known in spite of his country knowledge and natural cunning. The pheasants go scarce in what was a good covert and the talk in the public-house mentions Little Hugh as it might mention the fox when chickens are going astray.

'Hugh, boy,' someone will say, 'they tell me old Gower is losin' birds. Somebody's clearin' the place of them long-tails. He's kept watch, but never seen a thing.'

Little Hugh may take a drink before he speaks. His eyes will seem more blue and innocent than ever. 'There's all kinds of things after a pheasant,' he will say. 'There's fox an' stoats an' hawks an' whatnot.'

A Hare by Stealth

THE taking of a hare can be done in several ways. One may use a gun, a snare, a net, a pack of dogs, but all require the study of the particular ground. Little Hugh would favour a snare or net and Francie McGinn would want to shoot his hare, being a bolder character with more convictions.

The gate net – sometimes it is also used for partridges – is a thing designed for a hare. It is a little bigger in area than a five-barred gate, big enough to drape over the top bar and billow a little below the bottom one. It can only be used with real success after dark. When you want a gate net, learn the knots and make one yourself. I doubt whether you will buy one easily nowadays, and even if the iron-monger has them hanging in hanks you will be wiser to let them hang, for small talk in the ironmonger's shop will take word to the keeper and they will be waiting for you after a hare at night, or sneaking up on a covey when dusk has fallen. The night to use the gate net is the night when you can just see the clouds in the sky and yet not have enough moonlight to see the lines in your palm. If it is calm and still, stay at home, for the hare can hear the farm door closing and the bus labouring up the back hill out of the town when you can hear nothing but the beat of your own heart. Take a night when the light is right, for it will help you to escape without falling if you are discovered. If you go when it is as black as the under-stair cupboard, and the keeper comes across you by accident, you will stumble and clatter from here into the next county and probably be caught. There should be a breeze to cover your approach, a sound in the poplar tree like the waves on the shore, a whispering through the wood. Take half a dozen small stones and Little Hugh's dog, until I have told you about dogs and you have trained your own. The stones are to balance along the top of the gate, holding the net up and to keep it to the ground beneath.

When the net is in place you will lie a little to the side of the gateway; not too far away, for when the time comes you will have to be there to take the hare. Let your companion go quietly to the far side of the field with the dog and begin his walk. You can hear the thump of his stick and the sound of his boot striking a stone, and the hare you marked this morning can hear it too. He was somewhere in the field when you went quietly round stopping the runs. There is a piece of gorse blocking the hole through the hedge and another at the hole in the drystone wall.

He is moving nervously out there now, bouncing slowly along a draining hollow, uneasy, for he can both hear and smell the dog. They are closer to him. He wheels and goes off across the field, moving fast for the hole in the hedge. Now he has changed direction and is making for the hole in the wall. The dog has the scent of him. The hare has turned again. He is coming down the side of the wall more like a low-flying bird than a running animal. He senses the man and the dog coming across the open field. He swerves in an arc and comes for the gate. It is a silent thing. The net is moving gently in the breeze one minute and the next it is tangled about the hare. All you heard was the small stones falling and the soft scuffle. Be quick. Fall on him. Get him. Strike with the side of your open hand. Chop hard and break his neck. One clean blow and he is dead. Did you see the scurrying shadow? He had a mate. She went under the gate while you were laying him on the bank. Give the curlew whistle softly and get the net rolled, ready for the journey home.

The art of snaring a hare is in making sure that he will not snap the wire. With strong wire fast about his neck he has the power to kick so hard that the strands will snap. Some experts with the snare believe in twisting a thicker strand for a hare, but even set among rushes the snare may be seen. The real way to make sure of him is to set the noose up on its teal or pin, and tie the cord, not to a peg, but to a stone or a draining tile laid well back from the run, and concealed with grass or whatever natural covering is at hand. The hare will run into the noose and, when he kicks, the stone will give and bob a few feet with him. Before it has gone a yard he will be dead and spared the agony of struggle. Sometimes you can set for a hare as you would for a rabbit, but more often than not you will find the wire broken.

Francie McGinn, who cares very little who sees him, and who can walk faster over rough ground than many men over a smooth road, would prefer to shoot a hare. You must study the habits of the hare and note where he sleeps.

When the wind is blowing, get down wind so that the sound of your approach will be carried away, and walk him up. Put the dog from you, unless he is trained to your heel, or he may run forward to take the scent on the wind, and when the hare rises you may shoot the dog, as cleverer men have done. These are the ways of coming by a hare. Some may venture after him with a yelping of whippets, but they will oftener see the streaking brownness of him than hold him by the ears.

Finally, make sure you have a market for a hare. He is not always an easy thing to sell, for the womenfolk are not over-eager to prepare him for the pot. Carrying him, as I have said, take a grip of the ears, for this keeps the blood in the stomach so that it can be drained off for the making of soup.

The Ferret's Day

A DAY will come again, perhaps, when a ferret can be bought in the market-place. Many things changed when the rabbit plague came. The buzzard, they said, would die, the stoats would hunt in packs, hares would multiply and a great shift in the feeding habits of all kinds of predatory creatures would take place. Oddly enough no one said that the ferret would disappear. No longer would the cottager keep it in his garden shed, cooped up in a netted box to be brought out when he found a burrow to his liking. When the rabbit was the bread and butter of the poaching kind the ferret was essential. The rabbit, sleeping most of the day in his burrow, had to be persuaded out with the ferret. The would-be poacher must equip himself with a ferret, marking dog, purse nets and a short-handled shovel. Purse nets hang in the ironmonger's shop at this minute and a black rabbit eats the lettuce in my garden once again. Perhaps I may be excused for predicting that the rabbit will come again and that the ferret will multiply with it.

There are two kinds of ferret, or were, once upon a time. One sort was a little yellow beast with pink eyes that could slide in and out of burrows that tunnelled the bank with such speed that one had to be alert to note his whereabouts. The other was the brown and yellow polecat, a powerful beast able to fight and shift an old buck rabbit. The polecat, I believe, fathered the race of ferrets used by generations of rabbit-catchers. The wild polecat still lingers in secret places in Wales. The ferret cannot be gone if his ancestor is still to be found.

There was a day when I could take you to Anton for a ferret that would cost no more than ten shillings. Two ferrets are better than one. With two ferrets one can breed a strain of plucky hunters. Suppose that we are able, as once upon a time we were, to buy our ferret in the market-place or from Anton (a cruel man who would never make a string muzzle but tack the lips of his ferret together with needle and cotton to prevent it feeding on rabbit when put into a burrow ravenously hungry and eager to hunt). Take the advice of Little Hugh, I say, and make a pet of the ferret. Feed it well, but no better than you would a dog, or it will get fat and unhealthy. Get into the way of carrying it in your pocket, but be careful it doesn't wriggle out. Your ferret is as slippery as an eel and will often find a small hole in a sack that is tied at the neck. There is only one way of becoming friendly with the little hunter – handle him often. When you reach for him, calm your nerves. Let the motion of your hand be steady and deliberate or you will find him as firmly fixed to your finger as he might fix himself to the throat of his quarry, for he is nervous and excitable.

There was a time when burrows in the woodside linked others from here to the edge of the village, but the plague altered that. Only of late has the rabbit begun to rebuild his underground empire. It was said, at first, when the rabbit flea had spread the disease as far as it could, that the rabbit that survived was a new sort of rabbit, conditioned to life above ground, and it seemed that this was true. The rabbit ran the open field in the manner of the hare. This was to be expected. A small number of rabbits cannot rub and preserve the tunnels of a vast warren. It takes traffic to wear a footpath and it takes many rabbits to keep a warren open. With but a few rabbits coming and going the warrens caved in, the old burrows became impenetrable and the rabbits that survived disease lived in the open in folds of ground and such places. Now, make no mistake, the rabbit is returning to his ancient habits as his numbers grow. Soon he will be as safe as ever, in the labyrinth of warrens that undermine acres of land. It befits the man who buys a net and a ferret to know the ways of the rabbit and how to hunt him below ground. Take your new ferret along the hedge to the little warren with its dozen exits. Some people use a line and collar to enable them to recover their ferret if he blocks below, but the line itself may be his undoing when the little creature takes himself over and round roots and ties himself in his grave.

Hold him above the shoulders and put him down. He goes into the hole sniffing and showing interest. Stand back and say nothing. Watch the nets. It may be ten or fifteen minutes if he goes methodically through the warren, or he may show again in a few seconds. Put him back, for he has only worked a few yards. Hold your breath and take a look through the hedge in case the keeper is coming. Is every hole netted carefully?

The clock in the church tower chimed a while ago and

now it strikes the half-hour. When did he come up last? He showed at a hole-mouth for an instant. Was it near the gorse or up the bank? Perhaps he is blocked somewhere or he has killed and is lying up to eat, after which he will doze for the rest of the day. Lie down and put an ear to the ground. A sound of thumping? An old long-toothed buck defending himself? Steady. It seemed to come from over there. It is moving. Like a ball from a cannon the rabbit is up and the net is about him like an old woman's string-bag. Hurry and lift him. Break his neck as you did that of the hare and set the net once more. The ferret is out through the mesh. He seems to blink in the strong light of day, as though he had been down to the devil and back. Put him in again. He hurries back, wondering perhaps how the buck slipped past him down there.

Now he has startled the doe and she is sitting behind a net, petrified because he is creeping through the burrow with his musky odour drifting before him. Get her. Under the blackthorn there is an old hole clogged with leaves and we have missed it. That rustle was another escaping, crossing the bank and racing out over the field on the other side of the hedge. It is time to lift nets and put the ferret back in your pocket. Dusk seems to be crawling out of the wood and across the misty fields.

The nets you take ferreting will be new and white. Get a handful of soil and rub it into the cord so that it turns brown, otherwise the rabbit may see them and turn back, making the job longer. If you stand too close you will certainly frighten him, so stand away and leave it to the ferret. Keep the gun at hand, so that if the rabbit slips the net you can tumble him before he gets far.

Ferrets have a habit of blocking just about dusk. The afternoon is wearing away and you can hear the owl. It is colder and the excitement is waning. When that moment arrives and the ferret is below ground, look at your watch. As sure as you heard a cock pheasant call in the copse he will stay down and you have lost him. There are things called 'stinkers' for getting a ferret back; a kind of charm in their way. Block most of the holes and light a 'stinker' in one that is left unblocked. It should smoulder and in time drive out your ferret. It is sometimes a slow process.

If you do not starve the ferret to make him fierce, a practice as savage as the old country method of slitting a jackdaw's tongue to make him talk, he is not so likely to stay below, but if he does, there are one or two ways that may move him if he is near the entrance to a burrow. Take the rabbit caught earlier and push it into the hole, slowly withdrawing it again and repeating the performance. The scent and movement will bring him unless he has killed. If you have no rabbit, take a blade of grass between the thumbs and blow against it so that it makes a squealing noise. A ferret has the curiosity of his brother, the stoat, and will respond to the sound as he would to the squeals of a dying rabbit. He will even chase a twig if it is pushed into a hole and moved provocatively and he will come after it like an angry kitten.

However, no matter how fortunate you are in most things, the day will arrive when the ferret stays down. You will burn your 'stinker' and gorse, use the lure, thump, squeak and coax without result. Burrows extend according to the nature of the ground. The network may be eighteen inches below the surface or three feet down, going deeper through the roots of a tree. The digging will raise perspiration and mounds of earth.

In the company of two Welsh poachers I once spent a whole afternoon digging up a bank. We cursed the ferret in

the common tongue and I grunted my approval of the equivalents in Welsh. Just at dark, when we were agreed that he had gone as deep as we had wished him, we saw a glint of something white on the stubble. It was our ferret. Tiring of the noise perhaps, he had quietly sneaked out and was on his way across the field, running springily in the half light. We threw down our tools and made after him, but he skipped in the air and disappeared into a hole by a partly uprooted stump. It was too dark to do any more. We staggered back and fumbled for our nets and made our way home.

Usually when a ferret goes down and cannot be dug out its owner makes a despairing effort to block every hole with a stone, hoping to keep the ferret below ground overnight so that he is eager to come out when the holes are opened in daylight. Ferrets lie up when they have gorged themselves and seem as comfortable in the stuffiness of the burrow as a rabbit which stays down through a day-long rain-storm. Put down a lined ferret, some say, and the lined ferret, scenting the blood of the kill, will lie up with his mate; then all you have to do is to dig along the line. This process may mean altering the entire landscape, moving rocks and trees and going deeper than the brock, who loves the bowels of the earth.

Clever Dogs

THE dog that marked for us. Francie McGinn is the man for a dog. He can make friends with the fiercest dog and train anything with four legs and a tail. I walked behind Francie once. We were walking up a lane that passed through a farmyard. Francie did not know I was behind. As he reached the gate into the yard he gave his cur a signal. I dawdled, letting an elderbush screen me. Francie went on. The dog bounded up over a stone wall and went noiselessly through a rickyard. I reached the gate and went through. Ahead of me Francie slouched with his hands in his waist-pockets and a piece of sweet grass in his teeth. There was no sound, but, like a shadow, his dog came squeezing under a gate. Francie bent down and took the chicken from its mouth. In a moment he had the fowl in the lining of his jacket and was patting the dog when I reached him.

'A clever dog you have there,' I said.

'Infernal clever,' he agreed.

He did not say a word about the chicken. A feather tumbled from under his jacket. He shook his lapel and another fell to the dust.

'Infernal clever,' he said again, chewing on the grass. 'I've sold him twice, an' would you believe it, he come back the very next day both times!'

I wondered about the purchase money. Francie's money burned his pocket until he had a pint-pot in his hand.

The dog should be no bigger than a terrier and have courage and cunning. It should mark and hunt without barking. In the bar, just before closing time, when the imagination is stimulated and they are telling those stories of two-headed calves and the strange ways of rats stealing eggs, they will give you information on the ways of stopping a dog barking. Thrash him until he can hardly walk; put tobacco plug down the poor creature's throat; cut the end off his tongue. These are the men who will sew a ferret's lips or break off his fangs with a pair of pincers. It is a strange fact that these cruel theories persist even among men who are otherwise gentle and humane, considerate of the horses they tend, patient with the sickly lamb. Do none of these things. Pick a steady pup. Be firm but gentle and introduce it to hunting carefully. Let it get over its excitement and reward it when it responds. It must have a good nose. Two poachers will meet and stand for a long time looking at dogs, making proud claims for 'the nose' of their particular dog and its stout-hearted entry through gorse and blackthorn after an escaping rabbit. Your dog must have a strong constitution and, above all, must go home at an order when you run into trouble.

Once I borrowed a dog. His owner met me as I left for the woods and, seeing I had no dog with me, persuaded me to go to his cottage and ask his wife to let me have the dog. It turned out to be an old terrier of sorts, dim of eye and both slow and waddling in his gait. I could not refuse. The poacher's family stood about me assuring me in chorus that Spider would get me rabbits. We departed for the bracken and gorse slope. When I reached the end of the patch the old terrier was still fussing round a few sticks of dead bracken. I called to him but he remained there. I added deafness to my mental list of his infirmities, called again and then walked on. The dog did not come. I was out of gunshot when the pheasant rose from before his nose. He stood and looked at me in disgust. I took him home, stepped over the children playing at the door, and expressed my thanks and hoped that the old dog could not talk.

The pheasant can hear to-night's thunderstorm coming; the rabbit and hare can both hear and feel the vibration of your approach. The dog with a nose scents the partridge in the strong tang of the swede field, the rabbit in the heavy perfume of the gorse, the hare lying in the clover and the pheasant in the lower branches of the fir tree.

With a good dog you can go after rabbits with a gun, with purse nets or a long net. I have seen a man taking rabbits with only a dog and purse nets. On an autumn day, lured across the fields by the sight of a pheasant on a strip of new ploughing, I came upon a man and a dog in a hollow. They did not see me, for when I move I go quietly, keeping off the bare skyline and in the shadow as much as I can. He was a gipsy and his dog was a skin-and-bone whippet. When the dog marked a blackberry bush the man took purse nets out of his pocket and crept quietly round the clump draping nets over every exit. When he had done he began to bombard the bush with stones. A rabbit bolted and became entangled in one of the nets. Before it could struggle free the lean, long-legged gipsy was there, with his whippet keeping an alert watch behind him as he seized the rabbit and broke its neck. While I watched he caught four, and afterwards, when we met on the road, he offered to sell them to me at a ridiculous price, because, I imagine, I was wearing a new-looking coat and was therefore wealthy enough.

The Long Net

WHEN the rabbit multiplies, as it will in spite of all the confident talk of extermination, it will very likely become a preserved pest and part of the small farmer's economy as it was of yore. In days gone the rabbit which was said to keep so many farmers next door to the poorhouse was jealously guarded because it provided revenue from trappers or casual sport for shooting parties between more important dates. It was wild, but not entirely unwanted, and the law said it was a crime to shoot it without permission from the owner of the land. The fines were heavy and magistrates most firm in their enforcement of the law, as upright men should be. Had this not been so, the open country might have swarmed with rabbit hunters and more damage resulted from their depredations than a million rabbits might have inflicted upon the cropped fields. When the rabbit comes into its own again the long net will come out of the loft. At the moment no one goes by stealth to the woodside to set a long net. The setting of a net into which no wild thing plunges does nothing to make the spirit rise. The progression of the rabbit's reproduction needs a formula replete with symbols, but tomorrow, in the back end of the year, when the ground is firm and there is a nip of frost, it may be that you will feel compelled to go out with a long net. Like other ways of catching a wild creature it is not a business for fools.

I remember a friend who came by a long net – he moved into a cottage and discovered it in an outhouse – and talked two acquaintances into a night's work. They darned the holes in the net as well as they knew how, borrowed a dog and went to the public-house for a drink or two to give them heart, leaving the net, of course, behind a hedge in case the keeper happened to be taking heart in the same bar. When the place closed they staggered down the road and made their way across the fields to the woodside like a stampede of cart-horses. Two of them took fright at the threatening shadow of a small thorn tree and the third tripped and let the dog go free, whereupon the animal made for home in a streak of frantically working legs. The three poachers set up the net, struggling to unravel tangles and searching with matches for sticks that had dropped. One had to play the part of the dog, and when the net was up, off he went round the field giving out excited yelps that startled a flock of sheep. In ten minutes the feet of the sheep had dragged the net away from its pins, broken it and tangled it in such a manner that it was quite useless. The two who waited for the kill had retreated to the hedge, where they sat at the bottom of an ash tree and fell soundly asleep. In the grey light, walking home with the broken net, they were overtaken by a policeman, who took them in charge.

On my first expedition with a long net I was helper to Francie. He is a bold character. A long time ago he was chased by a keeper who fired a shot at him. The pellets of lead entered Francie's neck. They did no more than raise a few beads of blood. Some were hooked out by Francie's mother with a darning needle. The others remained. Francie is quite proud of them and he will ask you to feel them as they roll under his skin at the pressure of your finger, saying, 'Number four shot, them. Enough there to bring down a goose!' On another occasion, running at full speed down a ride in a wood, he tripped over a stretched wire and sprawled on his face. A second wire, set close to the first, cut him across the bridge of his nose. The injury so infuriated Francie that he waited for his pursuer and laid him low with the butt of his gun.

Francie and I took stable lanterns. A lighted lantern shows for miles, but we were on the secluded side of a wood and in the shelter of a hill. These lanterns were Francie's bravado. It is safer to work with a flash-lamp or a small lamp of some kind, for the storm lantern shows for miles when it has to be carried along the net so that the rabbits are dazzled and can be lifted quickly. I knew Francie hoped for some kind of excitement. We had three dozen rabbits at the first setting and had them in a sack and the net rolled, ready for moving on, when we heard a stone fall from a dyke. Francie stood out from the shelter of the wood, his outline a dark patch on the grey of the field.

'Haste you down the woodside an' away,' he whispered.

Groaning under my burden, I staggered off with the sack, the net and the sticks. Behind me Francie stood like a post in the field. Once I was safely on the road I put the net and the sack in the ditch and sat down to wait. Francie joined me in half an hour. He had walked around the keeper twice, he said, and had half thought of lighting the lantern I had left behind. I was thankful to get home that night.

An outing with Francie has excitement and real danger. He is the kind of man who prefers a bold march across an estate to skulking in the hedges. As he goes he watches for movement with the corner of his eye, quick to notice a figure making a line from a farmyard. Shoot and move on is his motto. Never stand where you have shot something, he will tell you, but get away out of it as quickly as possible. Yet he is not without cunning and he certainly has humour, for once he made boldly to a copse, where the keeper had been feeding pheasants, carrying a yard broom under his arm like a gun and a sack slung over his shoulder. On the way back he was pounced upon by the keeper and calmly gave up the sack of leaves he had swept up in the copse! A wild character if ever I kept one company, Francie is the kind of man who will insist on stopping to hold off pursuit while his companions get away. He has been in prison several times and is always penitent before the law.

'Bad company. I'm sorry,' he said once. 'Treat me fair an' I'll not be up again, I promise you. I wouldn't ha' been up now but for pure hard luck!'

The setting of a long net is a thing no aspiring poacher can master without the instruction of a man who has actually put down a net and succeeded in catching rabbits by this means. A long net may be seventy-five yards in length, and three feet or so in width. Threaded through the net are two cords, one at the top and the other at the bottom. At either end are steel pins which are driven into the ground and the net is supported by sticks a little over three feet long.

To run out a net requires skill. It must have been lifted in the right way on the last expedition or it will come out in tangles and half the night will be spent in putting it right. As a rule the first steel pin is driven into the ground by one of the setters while the man with the net retreats a pace, letting the first hank out of the great bag he wears round his neck. With the first hank comes the first wooden peg or stick. The net is drawn to the ground after the stick has been set up and the bottom cord is looped firmly round the stick. The second hank comes out; the net stretches twelve feet or so between each peg and the process of looping the cords and pushing the pegs into the ground continues until the full length has been set in a straight line. It is all done in absolute silence.

When the whole of the net stands pegged a final tightening and adjusting takes place, and then the dog, or one of the poachers, goes round the field to drive the rabbits in, and cover all the ground before the net. The dog must be one trained not to rush in after the rabbits or chaos will result!

As the rabbits strike the net the meshes bag up and hold him. There is enough slack to bag all the rabbits. The cords hold fast and the mesh is too small – about two inches square – to allow the rabbit to bolt through. One of the secrets is in knowing where to set and another in setting so that the wind billows the net away from the running rabbit.

Of Gins and Snares

No ONE but a barbarian thinks a gin trap a worthy instrument. The law has at last taken account of this feeling and the gin trap is beyond the pale. Many trappers depended on the gin for their living and regarded the trap as the most important item in their stock in trade. Had the outlawing of the gin not been coincident with the decline in the rabbit population I doubt whether its passing would have gone as smoothly. The gin, it could have been argued, was an efficient trap when used by an expert. It is true that it could not be persuaded to catch and kill in a humane fashion, but it caught anything that crossed its tongue and held what it caught, whether by leg, paw, nose, tail or belly. The trapper might be compelled to look at his trap within a given period of time but he could not be held responsible for the brutality of a device that belonged by rights to the days when men could be hung, drawn and quartered, when spring guns and man traps were used, and the lord of the manor kept his falcon. The gin trap will soon be a curio in the rural museum, but the really efficient trap that is also humane will not be seen until some genius incorporates an electronic brain into its mechanism.

As the wind blows the tree grows. The gin trap was a popular thing in the armoury of trappers and farmers in my childhood. An experience long ago taught me how brutal a thing it was. I had been searching through what used to be our cheese loft and came across a tin trunk containing a dozen old iron traps. They were the vicious-looking spring-handled type with serrated jaws and tethering chains strong enough to hold a sheep. Anton, on one of his mole-catching visits, had carried a few in his bag and had shown me how to set them by standing on the handle and carefully juggling the platform and tongue over one of the jaws. Without much thought I gathered them and put them in a sack, and the following morning, for it was late afternoon when I found them, I carried the sack to a distant hill.

There were holes in the hillside, but I preferred to set them in the runs through the stone wall. Down in the corner of the field there was a particularly well-worn path beneath a slab of stone. I had visions of a hare or at least a rabbit every day. I struggled manfully but found only one of the traps responding, because of rust. This trap I thrust into the hole in the wall, covering the platform with a few straws of dead grass, and proceeded to stamp the tethering peg firmly into the ground.

Next morning I arrived and got down on my hands and knees to peer into the hole before pulling out the gin. A hedgehog had been killed between the jaws. I released the body and reset the trap. The next morning I found another and on the third morning, becoming careless, I thrust my hand into the hole before looking, and the gin, which had been empty, clamped firmly to my wrist! The teeth, as

sharp as those of a farm dog, buried themselves in my flesh.
In agony I withdrew my hand and the gin came scraping
and jingling with it. I had not the strength to remove it
by depressing the spring with my hands, for even a grown
man must stand on it to release the jaws. I set to work on
the tethering pin, so well fixed in the stony ground. The
peg, too, was immovable. After ten minutes I gave up and
through my tears contemplated the trap on my arm. Little
trickles of blood from the cuts ran down to my finger tips
and splashed on my knees. I had an awful vision of myself
starving to death, tethered in the corner by the wall like a
goat, and screened by some of the tallest gorse for miles.
In imagination I lay at dusk, weak and with the mist forming beads of moisture on the wool of my jersey, listening
to the bark of the collie at home at milking time, shiver-
ing at the ghostly moan of the wind through the stones.

I was not just sorry for myself. I was more frightened
than I had ever been before. When I recovered my com-
posure I set my teeth and began the painful process of
moving my wrist in the gin. Every small movement
brought fresh tears. As the teeth of the gin dragged over
my flesh the skin was ploughed up. Several times I had to
stop and close my eyes until, finally, with the last rally of
my courage, I held the gin in my free hand and ripped my
other hand from its grip. The sight of my wrist, bleeding
and swollen, frightened me so that I could not look at it
again for a while. I stood up and made my way through
the gorse, leaving the trap, where it may lie to this day for
all I know. I never set another, and once shot a fox I found
tied down by one in the heart of a wood.

The man who invented the snare must have been as

pleased with himself as the man who invented the wheel. I shouldn't be surprised if the snare was devised a thousand years before the wheel, but almost its only modification will have been the use of a wire instead of a root or a thong. Humane or inhuman? Again it depends on the skill of the person using it. Like the hangman's art, it depends on the noose and how it runs. There are already enough rabbits on the hillside above my house for the snare to take a daily toll.

Properly set, the snare is the best way of killing a rabbit even if the business lacks a certain excitement. It is a thing a man does on a quiet afternoon when there may be a bit of a drizzle or a mist, wandering over rough ground where there are no sheep to become noosed by the feet. An old ewe can snap a snare with a couple of kicks, but in that time it may bite deeply into her slender leg and almost cut her foot off. Rough ground, dotted with gorse and patches of round rushes, is the best snaring place. You will find it criss-crossed with runs. On its way to feed, a rabbit will make deviations something like a hare, which seems to have a peculiar course, zigzagging and traversing from one side of the field to the other, first along the hollow of a sunken drain and then tacking back over a path all its own, like a ship sailing up-wind. An expert with a snare looks at a run and knows just where to set. He sees in the faint signs of flattened and standing grass just where the rabbit is on the jump and where he lands. He will set past the jump and the pear-shaped noose will be four fingers' width from the ground. This has to be judged, because a run will hold the scent of a man's hand.

The snare must not be too near the first setting, for if

one or the other catches, the struggles may frighten a rabbit on the adjoining run. A buck bounds into the noose and is dead in a minute, but a doe may squeal and her squeals attract a weasel or stoat, or even a poaching dog. There is a way of protecting the snared rabbit, a way as old as hunting. A hazel rod is driven into the ground and bowed down over the run. To the end of the rod a short piece of cord is tied, and this cord is also fastened to a notched peg as well as the cord of the snare. The notched peg is engaged in a notch in a pin in the ground. When the rabbit is in the snare its first movement frees the notched peg and allows the hazel rod to whip upright, carrying the snared rabbit up out of harm's way, where it hangs until the setter returns.

Once I saw a buck and doe running close together and, coming to a snare, both were noosed. Often rabbits run and brush snares aside because they were badly set or set at the wrong height. Little Hugh, an expert in all the methods of rabbit-catching, is fond of setting a snare in a wire fence. He sets at the point where the rabbit goes over or under the lowest strand and dangles a noose from a tethering pin twined in the higher strands of the fence. In this way he has more than once caught not only rabbits but an odd cock pheasant.

The beginner would do well to set no more than a dozen. It is not so simple as it seems. The runs may be fresh or they may be little used. The snare-setter has to know the rabbit and hare run from the path of the sheep, the run of the badger and the fox, or he will come to find his snare drawn out, snapped or swept aside by a lumbering beast twice as high as the rabbit. Every snare must be weathered. It is foolish to set snares that are freshly cut and whittled. After the tethering and setting pins are cut they should be buried in soil until they become stained. If they are simply rubbed with earth they will wash white in a night-shower. The best pins are to be had in a hazel thicket. Cut them and carry them away before trimming the points and slitting the tips to hold the noose. The gamekeeper may stand in the wood looking at your pile of chips and deducing that someone is getting ready for a season with the snares.

Before looking for snares it is as well to explore the field carefully. The gamekeeper has a habit of lying about waiting for a poacher to come and lift his snares. He will even go so far as to bait one if there has been no catch, simply to be able to catch the offender 'with a coney in his possession' as they say in court. There is nothing to do but to study the cover, look at the thorn tree, the patch of elderberry in the hollow, the mounds of gorse and the sheltering wall. Walk through casually and ignore the snares. Most gamekeepers are as fond of bed in the early morning as anyone else. Rabbits run at nightfall and at daybreak. It is useless to go before dawn. Better wait until the smoke is showing on the chimneys of the village and the milk lorry is crashing on its way along the back road to pick up churns from road-end platforms.

Remember to lay no more than you can lift, for you may have too many to reset and a heavy burden to carry. While you are stooping to adjust a pin the keeper may be coming with running strides from the hedge, his dogs bustling about him as he bears down upon you. As you make your escape you may have the misfortune to fall with your foot in one of your own snares, as Little Hugh once did. It is a business calling for wits. You must be more alive than the trio that crawled through the wood last night after roosting pheasants.

The cottager is fonder of snaring than any other way of poaching. He can slip from his back door and put down three or four without much chance of being seen. Isolated, he can take his time before going to look and need not worry about the gossip of his neighbours. If the stoat has been there before him he is happier, because he is less fastidious than the townsman. The rabbit he snares is for his own dinner, and the stoat only draws off the warm blood, leaving the flesh of the rabbit as white as chicken. Even the foraging magpie will take no more than the eyes. The dealer, however, will have no stoat-drained rabbits. A poacher selling his catch has many problems. If he sells to individuals he becomes too well advertised for the good of his business. If he sells to a dealer he may be betrayed to the keeper or the police if he refuses the price he is offered.

The rabbit, I have said, was the bread and butter of the poacher. Probably the rabbit has been the cause of more poachers going to prison and being fined than any other animal or bird. The poaching of rabbits gets in the blood of hundreds of country boys. The ragged youngster at the village school tries his hand at it as surely as he sets a line for the trout or goes gathering plover's eggs on a Sunday in April. The farmer's son is certain to do it more than once and even the parson's son falls to the temptation.

In the village on Saturday I would often see the poachers leaving. They would come home from work in a hurry,

gulp down a dinner and whistle for their dogs. There was a
nonchalance about them and you might not spot them.
One would wear an old raincoat and an earth-stained
battledress. He had a knapsack under his raincoat and only
the handle of his shovel showing from the sack he carried.
He might have been going to work in a garden but for the
dog running ahead and a certain look of excitement and
determination on his face. Another would be wearing a
coat tied at the waist with twine, and the bulges at the
pockets were purse nets on one side and a ferret on the
other. It would be dark before they returned and they
would sell their catch for the price of two jugs of ale. The
price of a brace of rabbits and a jug of ale seems to have
had some fixed relationship throughout the history of
poaching and drinking!

You might net a rabbit or snare one, but for enjoyment
the way to get them is to beat through gorse with a gun.
The rough shelters all kinds of things. The fox lies out on
the gorse hill, the partridges run to cover through the grass
and the bracken, the adventuring cock pheasant picks his
way through from one cultivated field to the next, the hare
lies out there and the rabbit can hardly be winkled from
the fastness of the boulders, gullies, mounds of hard, stony
earth and the impenetrable jungle of thorn and briar.
Nevertheless, pick a back hill and a windy day so that the
sound of your shot will be carried away like the bird flying
in the gale. Go in through the blackthorn across the marshy
patch and on up to the edge of the wood. When you have
shot twice, move on. Make for good cover and stand for
a long time listening. You will hear all manner of little
sounds, the timid chirp of the wren, the drumming of the

woodpecker and the sound of leaves drifting down to make a carpet on the ground. Listen to the distant cock-crow, the tractor buzzing in the field, the lowing of the cow, and distinguish from all these the sound of the gamekeeper's boot on the board of a stile, a heelshod against a stone, a cracking twig. Without a sound the small birds will come over, frightened by the keeper's progress along the path through the trees, a pigeon will burst from the top of a near-by fir and it is time for you to go, to go noiselessly as the fox skirts the place where a man is. The keeper has ways of knowing you have been in the wood. He will pick up your bright red cartridge case, noting whether it is weathered or not, and the bore, too. When you have fired unload the case into your palm and put it in your pocket, especially if you are using a poacher's gun, the folding four-ten, or one with a smaller bore than a twelve, perhaps a sixteen or a twenty.

One of the poachers in the village where I used to live had the habit of picking a time to go with his gun when no other human would venture. There would come a raw storm of hail, peppering furrows of autumn ploughing and beating the last leaves off the trees, or a downpour so heavy that it travelled across the fields like a sheet of glass and this man would put a scarf around his head, button his greatcoat about him and make for the wood and the comparative shelter of the trees, turning his back against the gale like a horse, bowing as the sheep seem to do. In the wood he might disturb a pheasant moving daintily to drier cover, or something equally attractive might come in on the sweep of the wind. Whatever he disturbed he would not move the neatly trimmed hazel rods the keeper left about so that he might know, if any were taken, that someone had been in the wood, and he would remember that it is habit that makes it possible to catch the hare, and a regular pattern of behaviour is the thing that brings a poacher to the dock.

A Partridge Whistle

BLACK BILL was already an old man when I was a child. I remember meeting him, or passing him at any rate, when I was being walked home from the 'preaching' at the country school-house one Sunday evening in early summer. My aunts had a firm belief that a preaching was a good thing for a small boy, if it only taught him to sit still and keep quiet for an hour and a half, and how hard it was to seem attentive to the preacher when, behind the school-house, the pigeons called through the wood, and close by its door ran a singing stream!

'Here's that character, Black Bill!' one whispered to the other as they hurried me along.

'He's a bit like Jesus,' I said solemnly as I took note of that character, and indeed he might well have been an apostle, for he had large soulful eyes and a curly black beard.

'Think shame!' my aunts scolded in unison and averted their gaze while we passed Black Bill.

I looked at him and he smiled; then all at once I lost his attention, for he switched his regard to a greenfinch that flew up and seemed to throw itself over the hedge. My boots squeaked as I plodded homeward. After a while I turned my head and looked back. Black Bill was hanging about a watering hole at the side of the road and probably observing a waterhen I had noticed there as we had hurried past.

'Well,' I said quietly to assuage the shocked religious feelings of my elders, 'if he's not like Jesus he's a bit like John the Baptist!'

'He's a good-for-nothing old poacher!' said one of them.

'He's a dirty old tramp!' added the other, 'and he catches little goldfinches and sells them, and The Lord will punish him!'

'He looked like The Lord to me,' I said.

For the rest of the journey home through the gathering dusk, under the ash trees, through the floating clouds of midges and up the footpath and over the stile until we came to the whitewashed farm with its peat smoke going up to the night, I heard the history of Black Bill, disciple of the devil, so they said.

Black Bill was a man for birds, they told me. He just naturally went after any kind of bird; the bantams of Willie Adair, the fowls of the schoolmistress, the guinea birds of Mrs McQuade, the little bird that sang in the tree and, worst of all, the pheasants and partridges in every wood and field for miles and miles.

'He's an ill character,' they wound up as we reached the farm kitchen, 'the like of which we wouldn't have about the place. Your grandmother once lost a setting of turkey eggs through Black Bill, the villain! Your grandfather encouraged him here, to spite the gamekeeper for something they had fallen out about, but he was glad to see the back of him, we can tell you!'

My grandfather had been dozing by the fire. He sat up
and lit his pipe, running a spill quickly through his fingers
to quench its flame as he always did.

'Black Bill?' he said. 'Black Bill can charm a bird off a
tree. He has the way of such things. He keeps a whistle in
his pocket and, when he's near a bird, he plays a bit of a
tune, I've heard.'

'He sounds a gentle man,' I ventured.

My grandfather laughed.

'A black-hearted, wild savage!' said one of my aunts
coming from down the hall, where she had been to hang
her coat.

It was a long time before I got to know the truth of Black
Bill, the man who could charm the little bird. I did not see
him again for ten years or more. By that time I had taken
to mooching the hedges with an old gun and had had the
lessons of Francie and Little Hugh to add to those of Jeck.

There is a time, just after harvest, when the ground
seems shorn, yet green with exposed clover; when the hare
is uncovered and runs in the sight of man and the partridge coveys are scattered more often. On autumn days,
before the first cold wind comes, the poacher begins to
take note of the movement of the partridges, listens to the
'two-thri' call they make at nightfall and thinks about the
net and the gun. I had been walking through a field of
roots, hoping to put up partridges, and came to the hedge
above the road. My heart bounded when I suddenly knew
I was being watched, and then relief came when I realised
that the watcher was not my enemy, the keeper. I looked
at Black Bill. He stood in a gateway, his hands thrust
deeply into the pockets of his over-large jacket, his black

head and beard a tousled tangle. I went to the gate and bade him good afternoon.

'I was looking for a partridge,' I said.

'A partridge?' He fumbled in his pocket and brought out a brass whistle made from the ends of two cartridges.

'Two-thri, two-thri, two-thri,' he whistled.

It was the call of the partridge collecting the covey, rasping, pausing and beginning again; the sound that was somehow dusk and the pathetic bleating of sheep when the last glow of the sun had gone off the highest hill. Black Bill's lips parted and showed remarkably white teeth while he whistled. Now he turned and swung his arm up, quietly pointing over the field. I caught my breath. Out of the ragged furrows of turnips a partridge ventured, inquisitive; a foot raised and held up, then delicately put down on the dusty earth; a movement through the motionless leaves and the straggling sorrel and another of the covey followed the first. They stood near each other, necks a little stretched, immaculate and beautiful little brown birds. I could only watch. I was no longer the poacher after a partridge. Black Bill looked at me. I shook my head silently. He put his hand to his mouth and removed the whistle from his teeth. The two partridges stood there. I could have killed them, but I could only think of what I had heard of Black Bill, who could lure the birds.

'Shoot them,' he said softly.

'A black-hearted savage,' I heard my aunt say.

'I couldn't,' I said and my voice frightened the birds, for they ran quickly up the furrow as soon as I spoke.

'I couldn't kill a partridge either,' said Black Bill. 'I could have shot hundreds in my time, thousands, yes!'

'I couldn't shoot them when they come like that,' I said, for I had my conscience and I had shot and eaten my share.

'A partridge to some,' said Black Bill, 'is just a little snack on a plate with gravy runnin' round it.'

'I've heard you're a bird-catcher,' I said.

He grinned through his whiskers. 'The partridge is the one bird I don't touch,' he said; 'but the old pheasant – now there's a proud an' impudent bird. I never spared one yet!'

We walked along the road together and he let me see his whistle. It was no more than an ordinary cartridge-case whistle, the kind of thing a poacher makes for his son to pass the time in the evening, and takes from him again in a day or so because the incessant noise is driving the family insane! I tried it with poor results. Black Bill explained that it wanted a great deal of practice. As we walked, the cry of a partridge came to us across a dun field of raked stubble. He put the whistle in his mouth and began to make the notes. It needed sharp eyesight to see the covey gathering. We stood a long time while the countryside fell asleep. The partridges came across the stubble, nearer and nearer to us, then Black Bill suddenly clapped his hands and they sank into the cover of the stalks.

They were gathered together, blending with the fawn and brown of the field, as motionless as they would have been had a kestrel hovered above them. I could have walked out and frightened them into flight but it seemed wrong. I followed Black Bill down the road.

Some time after this encounter with Black Bill I made myself a whistle and practised the 'two-thri' call. I was using the whistle to no obvious effect when Black Bill came out of a thicket where he had been setting up a trap-cage for a goldfinch.

'Wrong time an' the wrong day for that,' he said.

It was a damp day. A mist hung over the hollows. The rape and swedes were wet with rain that had fallen in the night. On such a day partridges keep to the ground and cry little if at all, and even at dusk, when a cold breeze hastens over the hill as though chasing the departing day they are silent. Such a day is one for walking the furrows with a gun.

On a bright day the partridges are out on the open stubble. Towards night, when there is a frost, they will be closer to the hedge, and even up among the gorse. An odd little call or two, somehow like two stones being scraped together, will rally the covey. In the bright autumn sun of the morning, Black Bill told me, the way to make sure partridges would not fly was to put up a kite, having marked where the covey was feeding. This is a job for two. One man flies the kite, and incidentally, advertises the thing to every sharp-eyed countryman for miles, while the other gets ready to walk to them with his gun. The partridges, at the first sight of the kite, freeze to the ground as they would for a hawk or falcon. They will then only rise when the poacher walks in among them and puts them to flight. It might seem a cruel deception, but not nearly so cruel as the method of Anton, who, having seen a covey in a turnip field, would run for his traps and set one in every furrow, after which he would beat down the rows with a stick and a tin tray. The birds, running ahead, would stand little chance of avoiding the gin and were caught in the biting jaws that crush their little bodies.

Elusive Coveys

On the wing partridges are fast. They rise in a flurry and are gone almost before the unwary man has time to cock his gun. They go whirring away down over the field swinging to the curve of the ground and planing down out of sight. Hasten to that very spot where you saw them land and it is most unlikely you will find one of them, for as soon as they are on the ground they run.

To hunt partridges you need Little Hugh's dog. These little birds have a strong scent about them. A good dog can mark them with no difficulty and, when he has marked, just consider the lie of the land. Ahead is a low hedge and to the left a line of trees. On the right a hazel copse and, behind, a long slope to a wood. When they burst up from the ground, as though from the muzzle of a gun, they will speed for the hedge and skim just over the top, dropping out of sight the instant they are over. They have not settled but are flying on, a foot or so from the field, or they will turn back in a great arc and shoot themselves forward down the slope. At the moment you think they will alight in the field, they will plane in through the trees, or even turn and seem to vanish against the background of brown soil,

dead bracken and the tufts of straw round the potato clamp.

The coveys of the quiet hills are even wilder than those of the lowlands. They rise quickly and speed off on the wind. They fly so far and so fast that you lose sight of them. You plod relentlessly on in the line of their flight and when you are exhausted they rise below you and throw themselves over a shoulder of the hill. The shot you fired echoes across the valley and you are disturbed to see the figure hastening up the footpath with two spaniels loping ahead. It is time to get out over the skyline and take the shelter of the march wall as fast as your gasping breath will allow. Away below, in the stony field where the hill farmer grew his potatoes, the call is sounding faintly as the wild covey gathers itself once more.

Remember that the partridge, like the pheasant, has a strong game smell. An acquaintance of mine who loved poaching carried his gun with him on his day's work at the plough. Turning over the old harvest field he drew near a covey and got ready. When he was near enough, he put them up and shot one with each barrel. At that moment he heard the keeper shooting two fields away and hurried to hide his kill. It seemed safe enough to raise the furrow and lay them under, hiding his gun in the same place and leaving a small white stone to mark the spot. This he did long before the keeper arrived, and he had, in fact, turned a second furrow beside the first before the keeper was in the field. Keepers, when they are not sure of themselves, affect a deceiving friendliness. They pass the time of day and ask casually did you hear a shot? Or have you seen anything of one of the notorious poachers? Perhaps you would like a rabbit for dinner? Careful! He waits to hear you say you can't face rabbit any more.

The man at the plough nodded his greeting and limped on a yard or two to the end of the furrow. As the horses stamped and jingled round, the keeper put his question. A shot? No. He hadn't noticed. The coulter glided into the soft ground and set up a new steaming paring of earth. The ploughman looked anxiously ahead, ploughing as though taking part in a match. Between the nodding heads of his team he could see the keen-scented spaniels doubling and turning on a scent, padding out over the furrows and returning; taking the message from the breeze, moving nearer to the buried game. The keeper's sharp glance turned from the dogs to the man at the plough, then he looked to the hedge for a hiding-place for a gun.

'A hare!' shouted the ploughman.

A hare had risen close to the feet of the horses. At that

moment the foremost spaniel had set his feet to the furrow where the partridges were buried. The keeper threw up his gun and the hare tumbled, then recovered and raced under the second shot. The keeper's whistle blew. The wounded hare tumbled again and yet ran on. The two spaniels, called off the furrows, galloped off on the hare's scent. The keeper lumbered after them, reloading his gun with one movement of a hand that carried two cartridges to the breech. The ploughman halted his horses and stood to watch. The man and his dogs disappeared through the next field. In ten minutes another shot sounded. In that time the partridges were out of the furrow and in the breast of the ploughman's shirt and the gun safely laid in a fresh furrow. The keeper and his dogs returned. The spaniels cast about, took the old scent and dug in the furrow. The keeper scratched his head and blew his whistle again and the ploughman smiled at the ears of his horses.

. The partridge makes her nest in the low blackberry bush at the edge of the field, among the dwarfed gorse, in the tall grass that will soon know the reaper. The brood run almost as soon as they are hatched, like all birds of the ground. The mother protects them from man and beast by appearing to have a broken wing, by seeming unable to fly and fluttering a yard or two and coming to earth, agitated and somehow bewildered. The unwary human hastens after her, two, three, four strides, and then she rises and flutters from him so that he hurries again to catch her. When he is lured away from the youngsters she will rise and fly out over the field, and in half an hour she will be back, clucking the brood together, weaving in and out of the tall grass very much like a domestic fowl. Long after they can all fly she will protect them in this way. In early October she may still trail a seemingly broken wing and invite death from the gun as she flies up and alights close at hand.

The real poacher does not bother much with the partridge. For one thing, the price of a partridge hardly repays the effort and guile required to come by one, and, for another, the hunting of a partridge must be done across an open field, arable land close to the farm.

Francie McGinn is a man fond of shooting partridges. He will go striding down a field of swedes or across a harvest field in a hurry, ready to shoot at the first movement, alert for the bounding rabbit, the running hare or the rising partridge. When he puts them up his gun will swing in a smooth movement, and almost always two will cease to fly in flight with the others and begin to roll and tumble through the air in a curve ending on the ground. The feathers they shed will still be drifting in the air after he has lifted them and hurried on for the boundary.

A man can become known as a poacher more quickly through shooting partridges than any other way. The farmer takes an interest in the covey and counts them. They are a thing he enjoys for his supper on a Sunday evening. Just like the poachers who will exchange information on the subject, he will remark, 'I notice there's only three in the covey on the little hill today. Did you see anybody about after them?' You saw the stoat hunting through the grass, halting and rearing, showing off the light hair on his belly, sniffing and turning his head, cunning and vicious. No, the stoat did not get them. The cock and hen are wary. They, too, raise their heads. They hear the rustle of the grass. Perhaps they get the odour of the stoat as well as the scent of the red clover. When they go, they move unobtrusively, hurrying across the bare patches with heads down, moving with new dignity when they cross the soft earth among the round rushes, upright, promenading, taking time to pick at an insect or a seed. The stoat did not get them, nor the cat. Perhaps the little owl, flying silently at nightfall, like a shadow, a ghost? Perhaps the little owl dropped among them? You saw the patch of scattered feathers? The brown and white feathers that form a heart on the breast of the bird? It might have been a bird of prey, for the carcase is gone, and there is no other sign but the feathers rolling and turning in the light wind, but more likely it was the crepuscular poacher who heard the cry and hastened over the brow to try a shot against the mottled sky of nightfall.

I have known poachers to keep a record of the number of birds in a covey and to hunt the covey at every opportunity until all the birds were in the hand of the dealer. Yesterday I heard of a poacher who sells them for three shillings and sixpence each and sometimes four shillings. Not so many years ago a hare was worth no more than two shillings – and partridges? I cannot remember, but pigeons were two for sixpence and now they are half a crown!

The dealer will turn the brace in his hand, pinch the breasts and click his lips.

'Poor things, these,' he will say. 'What price you want for these? They're no more than sparrows!'

You will name your price and remember that it makes no difference. Refuse, and he will tell the policeman you offered him game, and the policeman will ask to see your licence to shoot game. As though the fraternity concerned itself with licence! It is the very lack of licence that makes poaching. A man takes a licence for his mongrel, then a licence for his gun and the next thing he knows he is asking permission to shoot. When he is refused he is a poacher no more, but a tame villager who is in bed when the church clock strikes ten, every night of the week without exception!

Take the dealer's price. There was some reward in coming by the partridge. Some skill and cunning and not a little risk.

Getting a pair of partridges may take a poacher more time than he has to spare. The wind carried the sound of his approach and up rose the covey and away it went over the dome of the green hill; all at once one of the hens came out between two lumps of gorse and saw him before he was in gunshot, and her flight brought the rest winging after her, away across the meadow, diminishing in size and blending with the slope to which they sank with stretched wings and out-thrust necks. Little Hugh would lean over the gate and listen to the call of the cock bird, then look at the sky and nod his head, deciding to go for the net in a little while when the light had less strong reflection on the whitewash of the farm buildings and the first little glimmer of oil-lamps was showing in the windows of the village.

On the harvest field, where the clover aftergrowth is thick, the rabbits are almost buried. They have only to crouch and they are hidden. The man advancing only knows where they have hidden when the leaves of the clover hiss and flutter at the rabbit's frantic passage. In such growth the partridges could not feel safe to roost. Perhaps they are there when the sunlight is bright at midday and the leaves are dancing and the clover blossoms swaying, but towards evening, when their crops are full and they draw closer together for the night, they prefer the shorter grass of the pasture. On this field they can see the movement of the sheep and the grazing horse. The ploughman, short-cutting to his cottage, clumps past ten yards from them and they sit tight, almost vanishing into the ground. The stoat works his way along the bank, slinking into one burrow and out of another and misses their scent, or, if he finds them, they take a short flight in a half circle, alight and run a few yards, then walk with heads raised as they watch for sign of pursuit. The stoat lets them go, for he would wear himself away in chasing them. They close in again and seem to settle for the night. The owl glides out over the field in a slow, sinking wheel after a mouse or a vole and the partridges sit there like miniature chickens.

Hang on the gate, like Little Hugh. Let the light wane and the bat begin to fly about under the trees. Listen to the hollow sounds of twilight and mark the spot where the partridges settled when their brief walk ended. There they are, between the dead thistle and the tall weed. That little patch of uncropped grass, no deeper than the probe of a man's finger, hides all eight of them. A riddle would cover the lot of them. Begin, even now, to walk towards them and they will run or rise from the ground like an eruption, so sudden, so expected and yet unexpected, that its sound will startle you and they will be gone, settled somewhere else in the enfolding dusk. Look at the waterlogged ground in the hollow. When it is black and no longer reflects light;

when you cannot tell whether the shadow across the hill is a fox on his run or a hare bumping slowly over to the deeper gloom of the boundary hedge, they will sit still and make no attempt to move, unless your misguided feet carry you into the roosting place.

The netting of partridges is more often talked about than successfully carried out. It is not hard where the place in which they roost is clear of the hedge so that a man can walk between the covey and the hedge without disturbing the birds, when there are no little clumps of gorse, dead docks or hazel rods stuck in the ground to foul the net. It is not hard where a feeding rabbit does not rise and dash right through the covey. It is so easy under these circumstances that where they exist the partridges do not!

Every poacher with a reputation will give you his way of netting partridges. Remember the covey sits still in the dark. A rabbit will run and a hare too, but a partridge is snug in the darkness. A careless searcher would mistake its feather blending in daylight. In the night it is safe, so it need not run unless the thing disturbing it is close at hand, and then it will hurl itself into the air, into the vast space of night where you have no more hope of netting it than the curlew that flies high in the darkness making its lonely cry. Mark the spot, they will tell you, and look out for the obstacles placed in the field to prevent netting, the thorn branch and the gorse fragment to become entangled in the net being drawn across the field. Look out for the sheep, the ewe and her grown lamb dashing side by side between you and your companion. Let three of you go, they will advise, and the third man can disentangle the net, lifting it over the obstacles so that progress can go on.

This I can advise, for I have tried my hand at the art: the fewer engaged in the job, the quieter will be its execution, so let no more than three of you go. You have marked the roosting place. Take the twenty-five-yard net that hangs in the stable or the shed. Examine it in daylight, see that your weights are tied along one side of it, then, at nightfall, carry it stretched between you, holding it as taut as you can. At every step you will know if the tight net has encountered a thistle or a twig. Draw it high at first, then draw it lower as you approach your landmarks, the dark shadow of the hollybush in the hedge, the fence-post in the other boundary. As the net comes the covey may try to rise. You will feel it all and learn how to handle the net. It is not easy. A fool can put a rabbit out of a burrow with a ferret, but it takes a wildfowler to net partridges. Like netting a hare, it is a thing that is either successful or a complete failure. The expedition begins at nightfall and it is over before the farm dog has stopped his barking, before the fox has crossed from the thicket to the wood. At its end you have either a covey in your bag or you have nothing but a point or two to add to experience!

Little Hugh, a man of great patience, will have his net in readiness. He will decide whether the birds settled where he saw them last or ran for the engulfing gorse. When he has considered all these things he will put his feet in seed bags to muffle his boots and bid you do the same. He will speak no more until it is all over, and there will be no dog either at your heels or his own! You will know Little Hugh well before you share this enterprise with him. When it is over he wants the birds in his hands and to ensure it you will have to co-ordinate your movements with his, understand what he is doing without seeing him, become a poacher in the true meaning of the word.

These are the only ways I know of getting partridges: use a gun or a net, or, like Black Bill, blow a whistle or fly a kite so that they keep to the ground to be taken by walking up and shooting. Anton, as I have said, will set traps. I heard of a man who put little steel traps in the dust where partridges were in the habit of taking a bath, fluffing their feathers and basking in the sun. There are cruel ways and ways less cruel. Partridges are such handsome, dignified little birds that it seems a pity to harm them. They are preserved as game because they are tasty on the plate and slaughtered by the dozen couple when the shooting party goes through the turnips and over the hill. It is said that they are a difficult shot and fly very fast with the wind. The poacher never shoots a dozen couple or nets half that number. He takes what the fox might take, what the hunting stoat might take, by wits and cunning and with less regularity. To him, as Little Hugh might say, they are no one's birds until they are in the hand of him who can catch them.

I remember watching a covey on a September day. It had been very hot and I was in the cool of the farm kitchen, seated in my grandfather's arm-chair and gazing idly out of the window at the little field where the beehives sat. Among the beehives I suddenly saw the movement of a partridge. It was so near the house that I caught my breath with surprise. The hen partridge led her brood through the white bee-boxes and down the grass past the chickens that were sitting in their hollows at the hedge bottom. The guinea-fowl ignored them and a cat sprawled on the grass looked at them and went on washing its paws with its tongue. I thought of Sunday evening supper and looked at the gun leaning against the clock. All at once my attention was taken by the partridges again. A long-legged, scrawny chicken stalked slowly towards the covey. As she drew near the hen partridge she shot out her neck and pecked. The partridge ran and the covey followed at her heels. The chicken gave chase. Round the first beehive they went. The partridges twisted and turned in unison. It seemed as though they were tied together by fine thread. The winding chase went on for a minute or two and then the covey seemed to tire of the game, for as one they rose and threw themselves over the stone wall in a short flight that left the domestic fowl frustrated. When I went out with the gun a little later they were gone and I was glad.

Longtails

THE partridge, our native little brown bird of the fields, is declining. Shooting men have said this for a long time. In Ireland when it declined it was forbidden to shoot the bird. Whether this brought it back in reasonable numbers or not I do not know. If we protect our partridges by forbidding anyone to shoot them for a season or two it will be doubtful whether the bird's future will be affected. It is a native and it belongs on the rough hill as well as the cultivated plain. It may become as scarce as the corncrake, but shooting partridges as a sport has fostered and sustained the bird in places where it might not have managed to hold its own. Like good trout, the partridge passes through cycles favourable to its breeding and general condition and it has its bad seasons when it declines, drowning in ditches and waterlogged meadows, being killed off by parasites. The pheasant, on the other hand, is a thriving bird. There is rarely talk of its decline for the simple reason that it is extensively bred and artificially fostered on land that is well-keepered. It is a pampered bird, it is a handsome bird and it has always been more eagerly taken to the kitchen than the little partridge for the simple reason that there is more flesh upon its bones. The man who shoots game for his amusement turns oftener to the pheasant for his sport than to the partridge. By the nature of things generations of poachers have been punished for attempting to live off the fat of the land in the form of the long-tailed bird.

The ways of coming by a pheasant are numerous and legendary. Some of the ways are dangerous and some of them are ways practised by poachers only when they have an ale pot in their hands and a warm glow inside. When I was a youth the keeper in the locality was convinced that I shot sackfuls of his pheasants in a season, and told our neighbours that he had seen me knocking his birds down time and time again; but I was sixteen and he was seventy. There was truth in the difference in our ages, but he had cunning and experience if I had fleetness of foot, and I always felt I owed it to him to do my best to make his exaggeration of sackfuls of pheasants less of a lie than it was.

We developed a strong mutual hatred of each other. He would send messages to me through a relative.

'Tell him,' he would say, 'I saw him Tuesday afternoon on the turnip hill. I saw him put the cock down. If I catch him he's for the court!'

To my disgust and shame, my relative who was friendly with the keeper would give me a lecture on the errors of my ways and the danger I ran. These lectures had little effect. I shot nearer and nearer the keeper's lodge, where he had a wire-netting enclosure in which he fed a number of almost tame birds. One day, in defiance, I took a shot at a group of birds through the netting, believing the keeper to be away elsewhere on the estate. The shot was not so much intended to kill pheasants as to give the keeper news of my boldness through his wife, who was in her garden at the time. The report of my gun had hardly died when the lodge door flew open and the keeper came lumbering out. I turned and ran. Somehow he drew closer than I had expected and I found myself running uphill in a firwood with the old man about seventy yards behind. Before I reached the top I slipped and tumbled back. The distance between us shortened alarmingly. I could see him panting up after me as I clawed myself upright and tried to run again. Perhaps he had exhausted himself and saw that, close though we were, he could never overtake me; perhaps he grew desperate and more enraged by the feebleness of his years, but as I scrambled on I heard the roar of his gun and a second or so later I felt something strike my neck. No rabbit was ever more frightened. I fell and put my hand to my head. I hardly dared look at it to see the blood from the gunshot wound, but when I looked I saw my hand was not marked by my blood as I feared. New heart came to me. Before he could fire again I was through the trees at the top of the ridge and going like a deer down the other side, leaping over gaping warrens and roots, escaping as I had done countless times before. The spattering feeling on my neck had been caused by fragments of fir twigs coming down upon me as the keeper's shot tore through the trees high above!

Two friends of mine who were chased by a keeper ran through a park carrying a gun and a sack containing four birds, and were accompanied by their lurcher. When a second keeper joined the first and a car began to race ahead of them down an adjoining drive, it seemed certain that they would be caught. One swung round and ran off at right angles to the original flight, and the other turned to give battle. The two keepers separated. The running poacher, who carried the sack and gun, became the quarry of one of the keepers. The poacher who stood his ground gave a signal to his dog. It ran in quickly and snapped at the heel of the keeper's boot and over he went. The second keeper hesitated, and the poacher broke back past him. He turned to give chase and the lurcher somehow ran in between his legs and brought him down as he had the other. The first poacher was by now well into the shelter of a nearby wood. His companion whistled up the dog with two fingers and ran on, and soon he too was in cover. The same evening when I met them they were laughing about the dog. It seemed that the dog had been taught the game by the children of one of them, and had become a bugbear in the village for the habit of up-ending anyone who ran or moved fast. It sobered them both a little when I remarked that it was a good thing the dog had not chosen to turn play-ful with either of them while the keepers were in chase.

It is not an exaggeration to say that on some estates the keeper has his pheasants counted. He walks through a field in the late afternoon and watches the cock and his plurality of hens running for cover. He makes a note of one cock and four hens in the thicket in the hollow. Next week he may note that he has gathered another hen. He will also note that the cock came out alone when he walked through the thicket and that two odd hens got up from the blackberry tangle on the far slope into the hollow. It reads like a book to his experienced eye. They have scattered, badly dis-turbed, and perhaps two hens have fallen. Certainly one has gone, for he saw the wad of a cartridge on the open field and a few yards away some feathers sticking in the mud, and the imprint of a hobnailed boot.

The whole world is quiet, blanketed with chill mist. In among the beech trees the leaves are damp. The thick barrier of the spruce-planting gives out a resinous smell. Out on the green of the field the pheasants are feeding, a short run from the dead bracken, so near a matching shade for the plumage of a hen or a cock pheasant.

The keeper hangs about. Yesterday at half-past three he heard the report of a gun. He is in the clear patch below the towering dead tree. Like the pheasant, his dress is a blend with the brown and grey of the wood. He hears the fence creak and the little sound that might have been a man coughing into his hand. The pheasants hear it too. They are no longer picking among the grass. The cock bird has his head raised and the hens are intent on the small sounds and vibrations. They do not run. There seems to be no hurry, but they fade from the field. They are in the bracken, steering through the fallen elm and the débris of broken branches, up over the bank that is riddled with rabbit holes and on under the awning of bracken that has fallen on other dead branches and twigs.

The poacher is on the far side of the field, a figure hard to see, for he is standing close to the oak tree with a hawthorn behind him. He did not see the pheasants go off the field. He looked for them within yards of the spot on which they fed, but his eye caught the pigeon gliding out over the fringe of the wood and he saw it loop up and go in fast flight back in the direction from which it came. It was all too far away for him to have seen the keeper or his dogs, or for the pigeon to have sighted him by the oak tree, although the pigeon has eyes keener than the hawk. The pigeon was no more than a dot. To the man who has not studied the characteristic flight of birds it might have looked like a pigeon, a crow, a magpie or even a fieldfare. Its turn in flight from a glide to fast-beating wings could have indicated a hundred things and none of them the right thing, but the poacher knew in that instant where the keeper stood, and the keeper knew too, when he heard the clatter of the pigeon's wings, that if the pigeon had been observed, the poacher was moving away with the same noiseless stealth as the pheasants.

The poaching of a pheasant by day is a thing of stealth or great speed. The wind is blowing and making the whole wood rock. It has blown since the earliest hours of the morning. The crossed limbs of an ash and gangling thorn squeak and groan, and dead fir-cones rain on the grass and the path. The pigeons, carried across the undulating country by the buffeting wind, sweep in and take bobbing foothold on the top branches of tall trees from which they can keep watch. They are more nervous because in the wind the warning is carried away unheard. They love the hollow stillness of the watery sunset when the smallest noise resounds through the drum of the wood. Now they sway aloft there until they tire of their vigilance and take a short heavy flight to the sea of thick fir-tops.

Like the pigeon, the pheasant loves the echoes, and the quiet day when the tractor purrs a mile away and the sound of children playing about the farm carries clearly across the acres of sleeping land.

On this day, with the wind making your eyes sting and its hands plucking at your clothes, take the shortest route across the fields and hurry along the hedge-side. That gully round which the three elms stand is a likely spot. The pheasant cock with his attendant hens went down to the little stream, moving through the two patches of gorse. The last dead leaf comes whirling past you as you go towards the trees. Put your finger on the hammers and gently ease them back so that both triggers are cocked. Get ready. It is a strange thing, but somehow at the instant of your appearance they will know you are there and become for a moment so motionless that you will not see them though they are in the centre of your vision. Their rising will not coincide with your own coming to life. Put up the gun and shoot, right, left, and the thump you heard was one of them striking the ground behind the gorse. Hurry forward with the dog, for the bird may only be winged, and already racing up the knoll and over to the cover of the wood and its undergrowth.

Study the pheasant and its habits. Early in the morning when the sun is a streak of light in the east and day is only half-arrived, with the fox no more than settled in his lair, the pheasant moves gingerly out over the old wheat stubble. There is no gamebird with hearing like his. In the growing light he feeds, walks a little way, listens and walks again, and cover is always close at hand. When he is with his harem he will be lulled a little, and venture farther into the open field, but split from them, perhaps by the last raid of the shooting party, he will be cautious. No nervous hen will save him the anxiety of having to take a morsel and listen twice. Watch him from the shelter of the hazel copse and the screen of blackthorn draped with rakings from the side of a harvest cart. When he vanishes you will know that you betrayed yourself by some unconscious movement that carried warning in sound so small that you could not believe it would reach him. Walk out with your eyes fixed on the spot where he was. If he can see you as well as hear you, he will run a few feet and launch himself into the air with great speed and sound of thrashing wings. He will look heavy and a grand target until you miss him. If he does not see you he will stay where he is until you are almost on top of him, or until you have blindly walked past, and then he will go with a suddenness that will paralyse your movements while he puts yards between you and his magnificent red, white and chestnut-brown body.

In the afternoon, in the scent of mustard and swedes, you will see him for a brief instant between the rows, the spear of his outline vanishing between leaves that flutter and bob and rustle. You will begin to walk. Every stride will make you more excited, and while you walk he will run. At the end of the field he will speed up the bank and into the tangle of rose and honeysuckle, and on, over the cart-track, never bothering to reveal his escape by the noise of his wings.

In the undergrowth of the thicket you will be startled by the sudden rustling of leaves and a scurrying like a rabbit breaking out. This is not the habit of the rabbit. When you are close and he is in cover, he crouches, and, when you have moved a little way, he hurries noiselessly off, but the pheasant cock becomes uncomfortable at your proximity and runs. You have little hope of seeing him. In a moment he is in the dry ditch and away without more sound, or the rustling passes into the next clump of briar and dead bracken, across the wet ground where the alder grows, and over the leaves and beech mast, and ends with the whirr of his wings and the alarm call sounding across the adjoining field.

Hurry to the fence. He towers yonder above the stunted

ash and the elderberry, and then drops, yes, drops for all the world like a hen fluttering heavily from a spar. The undergrowth is thick about him. He runs downhill now, across the mouth of the badger hole, past the badger 'hay' that lies where the badger scratched it out when last he cleaned house, under the drooping nightshade and past the wild raspberry canes, until the memory of your intrusion in the thicket grows faint and he begins to pause, pick and listen once more.

At dusk he will come out of the tangle, for his scent is strong, and the fox is hungrier when the frost is in the late autumn air. His enemies would find him and he could not outrun them, or rise, for the tangle above would bring him down to the snapping jaws of the grizzled badger or the fox. Before it is too dark he will take flight again, across to the thicket or the firwood, and fly into the lower branches of the tree to roost. There he is, not so high as the pigeon or the crow perhaps, but you must learn to recognise him. The gloom below is a comfort to him. Night settles in about the fir tree the holly bush and the thorn, and he is safe.

Bold Characters

Some of the boldest characters are those who poach pheasants, for it requires boldness both by night and by day, unless you have the gift of Black Bill and the cunning of Little Hugh. It was always said of a keeper I knew that he spent the night in bed when a gang of local poachers conveyed the information that they would be after pheasants. The landlord would lean across the bar and in a confidential whisper tell him, 'Some o' that lot is after the birds tonight. Thought I'd better tell you.' The keeper would nod his head and scowl, then go quickly out to his bicycle and ride home, so that if official warning came in the night he could always give the poachers a chance to get away by the fact that he had to dress and put on his boots before giving chase! Gangs of poachers, banded together for protection and a large return in cash, do not hesitate to fight their way out of a tight corner, and if a gun goes off in the dark, it may be aimed at a roosting pheasant or the keeper of the pheasants!

Black Bill, whose eye missed nothing, never failed to get pheasants without a gun. His method was an old one. In the middle of a small wood he would construct his own hedge of sturdy twigs. These would be set so close together that they formed an impenetrable wall for a pheasant, but at intervals he would leave small gaps and in these gaps he would hang nooses, or small snares. When the thing was nicely constructed and the snares set, he would go home. The following morning he would return to beat through the wood with the sound-making device of two sticks which he struck against each other. The pheasants on his side of the barrier would run quietly and unseen to the twigs and dart through the gaps to be snared as neatly as rabbits. When he lifted his catch and reset his wires he would make a wide circuit of the wood and enter it again from the other end, tapping his sticks and walking to the long barrier. In this way he would clear almost every pheasant that did not rise and fly. Not only would Black Bill set wires in an artificial hedge, but he observed the runs of pheasants, the places where they passed through a natural hedge, going under a branch or through a clump of bracken.

Little Hugh had an old shotgun cut down for the purpose of shooting roosting pheasants. He would take this abbreviated gun, easily concealed because of its shorter barrels and trimmed stock, and creep into a wood at night-fall. When there was no moon he would use a torch, flashing it on and directing its beam into a likely tree. The gun, having been cut off at the pistol grip of the stock, he could use in the same way as a pistol, which enabled him to hold the torch in one hand and aim with the other. He was very proud of this method until he was caught and his gun confiscated.

I remember the first time I tried by moonlight. I shot three old crows one after the other, and dared not remain in the wood any longer because the intervals between my shots had given the keeper ample time to locate me.

Go with Little Hugh. He will impress upon you that you must keep your ears open, that you must not mistake an owl for a pheasant, or shoot unless you are sure. He will hold the light and direct your shot because he knows where to look. You might go to the bleak north side of the planting or the open trees, the tall and bare beeches and elms, but Little Hugh will take you to places where he knows the birds roost, and his knowledge is from observation as well as instinct. The shadow in the tree is one of his specialities. When the torch goes on and you fire, a pheasant will fall or Little Hugh will seek an accomplice who 'shapes like the thing'.

The first time you take a share of a bag you will want to eat one yourself, and this may lead to your undoing. The feathers, blowing about your garden will give you away to the keeper, so you must hide them. Pluck the bird into a bucket of water, dig a hole and pour the soaked feathers into the earth and cover them over with soil. Once, knowing the importance of hiding game feathers, I plucked a bird into the fire. The following day I suffered anxiety because pheasant feathers blew round about the house, on the garden path and among the leaves of our privet hedge! They had been carried up the chimney by the hot draught in the flue and spilled themselves down the roof for the whole world to know I had been poaching again!

With a keeper hard on my heels I once bolted into the farm kitchen, carrying my gun and a brace of birds. I looked desperately round for a hiding-place, knowing that the keeper, although he had no right to do such a thing, might dash into the room after me. One of my aunts, anxious for my good name, and with a little of the family devil in her, perhaps, pulled open the door of the grandfather clock. I dropped the brace inside, laid the gun in its usual corner and flopped in a chair at the moment the keeper knocked loudly on the door.

Hospitality had never been refused even our greatest enemy. My aunt opened the door and invited the keeper in without asking why he was so out of breath and red of face. Would he have a cup of tea? I controlled my breathing a little better and bade him good-day in what I thought to be a casual voice.

'Pheasants?' I asked.

He blustered and accused. I brazenly said he could search if he wished, but he stalked out, rudely refusing the tea my aunt offered. He had hardly crossed the threshold when the weight of the clock ran down, and instead of striking the bottom board with a crash it softly thudded on to the pheasants!

On another occasion the same keeper paid my grandfather a visit and sat on our settle-bed. Under him, hastily transferred out of sight from the hook in the ceiling-boards, were two partridges and a hen pheasant. As a rule, however, game was kept out of sight in the long, cold cupboard under the stairs where my grandmother matured her blackberry and elderberry wine. There was even a time when I became so notorious that gun and cartridges were kept there too, and the story went about that my grandfather had sold the gun to force me to mend my ways.

While on the subject of hiding-places for birds and the disposal of feathers, remember that pheasant or partridge are better hidden up from the ground. Tie their feet together and hang them on the coat-hook, covered by an old jacket. Your dog or the dog of a visitor will be less likely to scent them up there, for the air rises from the floor and carries the scent to the ceiling.

Whatever bird you shoot, you will learn a great deal about his current feeding habits by examining his crop. Look at the crop of the pigeon. He is on the stubble of the wheat in September, among the oaks and full of acorns in October, nibbling at bits of green stuff and hedge berries later and among the first shoots in early spring, the sprouting pea and the 'bread and cheese' of the hawthorn. In the same way you may learn where the partridge searches for food, and the fact that the pheasant is being fed wheat or oats in some sheltered glade known only to the keeper. Wherever the pheasant lives there will be water, a streamlet or a ditch, cover close at hand. Like the keeper, you can set up as a feeder of game. Get yourself a small bag of corn and fatten your birds as Little Hugh and other poachers like to do.

Baiting the ground is an old and favoured way of getting game. The keeper does it to ensure birds in certain parts of the estate just before a shoot is to take place, and if it works for the keeper, it works as well for the poacher. A bag of tail corn left by the thrashing-mill is good enough for attracting pheasants, but it must be scattered in a suitable place, perhaps along the side of a wood or in bare patches in a stony hollow where the birds have been seen on a bright autumn day. Like snaring, or prowling the wood in the moonlight, it has its dangers. The keeper knows that corn and chaff does not come into a lonely field at the back of a hill by accident. He knows where the pheasants are, and in such places he makes his rounds, so that when you bait ground with corn it is as well to reconnoitre the locality every time before making another sowing.

Francie's method would be to lay the corn for several days until a good enough number of birds were congregated to feed there, and then he would creep up with his gun and let go both barrels into the thickest mass, hoping to kill three or four. Little Hugh, as great an expert in another method, would change his bait on the last day and return in time to lift his intoxicated pheasants.

I have not seen this carried out, but I know the potent effect of a drop of spirit on a canary! We had a canary once. He sang all day in a cage above my grandfather's chair and his song was taken for granted, while, like the

collie dog and the black horse, he grew old. One day it was noticed that he had a 'wheeze' in his chest and the next he took to falling off the spar. A drop of whisky worked wonders for any member of the family who caught cold. Might it not work wonders for Joey? One drop in his water dish and Joey revived. Two drops for insurance, as it were, and Joey became intoxicated, swayed and closed his eyes and generally behaved like an inebriated canary. Often I have promised myself that I will try making pheasants drunk, but baiting requires patience not to be wasted by any method likely to prove sterile in results.

Black Bill, the man with the way of birds, always knew a novel method. He would bait under cover, in the tunnel between a thorn hedge and a field of gorse, in the shelter of a hazel copse, among the dead grass and sleeping roots of primrose and wood anemones. His bait would be corn and raisins, and after the second or third day there would be more raisins and less corn, with a fish-hook in every raisin! A pheasant must be able to raise its head in order to take off. It cannot fly if its head is held to the ground by a short length of brown line attached to a rod. Black Bill would fasten ten or a dozen hooks to a rod. Walking among the grass in search of grain and the tasty raisins it had yester-day, the pheasant would take the raisin and hook in an instant and remain attached to the rod until Black Bill called back. There is cruelty and cunning in this method. The bird which swallowed the bait could not escape with the raisin in its crop, nor could it disgorge it without drawing away from the rod. When this happened the hook would slip through the raisin and fasten itself in the lining of the crop so that escape would become impossible.

Legends

THERE are other ways belonging to the legends on taking pheasants. I have heard of them often enough without ever coming across the man who has actually used them. Perhaps he died a long time ago, or did he only have an hour of glory when those about him gasped as he expounded his cunning?

·'Ah,' they will say, 'there's more ways of killin' a cat than feedin' it on cream. . . .'

If you are to believe this story and prove the effectiveness of the method, you bait the ground with wheat or hard peas. When the birds have become accustomed to feeding in your selected spot, go to the stable and pull some of the long hairs from the mane of the mare. Watch she does not turn and snap at you as you jerk them out! The hairs are selected with some care. They must be long enough and stiff enough. A hole is made in the grain or the pea by means of a pin or a fine needle and the hair threaded through this hole. Every piece of bait is threaded on to a strand of hair and the bagful taken and scattered where yesterday's bait was laid. The voracious pheasant will gobble down the first grain of wheat or pea, and the hair will protrude from his beak. He will gulp and wipe his beak on the ground, strike at it with his foot, first the right foot and then the left. The urgency to remove the hair will become desperation and in the end the pheasant will fall down, still striking at his beak in a frenzy until he is exhausted. The poacher will return in the afternoon and find his birds lying about, unable to fly, unable to rise, incapable of anything except the feeblest kicking of one leg at a head that distinctly wobbles! They can be lifted and bagged with ease!

I do not guarantee this method. Some ways of coming by a rabbit, pheasant, partridge or hare require skill, and some, like that of sending a tortoise down a burrow bearing a lighted candle-stump on its back, so that it may drive out rabbits, require no more than credulity.

Another method, and I cannot vouch for it, or even claim an acquaintance who has used it, is the use of rock sulphur. The poacher buys a quantity of sulphur and puts it into a large tin in the sides of which he has punched a number of holes. The sulphur can is carried to a wood. The moon must shine or the poacher must have a torch or lantern. There must be a good breeze, not a wind, for it would defeat the object. The sulphur is set on fire, and the can or cans are placed so that the fumes carry on the breeze into the trees. A whiff of the sulphur fumes will overcome a pheasant in a minute or two and the poacher has no more to do than to pick them off the ground, having thrown a sack over his gas-producing outfit.

For my part, I have always favoured the straight-forward way of getting a pheasant: a shot and a walk in the shelter of a tall hedge or through a wood.

In the idle days, when the poacher has no income and has to concern himself with a day at harrowing or muck-spreading, cleaning a ditch or burning couch grass, the partridges are pairing and flying in pairs, rising quickly and sailing over hedges in short flights, and the cock pheasant is gathering his complement of young hens. Yesterday, when the wheatear was on the harrowed furrow, the pheasant rose from the hedgeside and went down in the thicket in the hollow. The late lambs have come, and the bluebells are in the wood where there is warmth and crackle of heat that makes the man on the footpath think of the gliding grass snake and the basking adder. The pheasant is nesting. There, in the clump of gorse, by the tangle of old fence wire and the stones gathered from the field to fill an idle afternoon, the hen sits tight on a nest of fawn eggs. See the proud and richly marked cock going down across the muddy patch at the brook and those eggs seem small for such a fine bird, particularly after you have seen the sharp-pointed large egg of the curlew, or even the plover's clutch on the brown earth where the oats were sown. The hen pheasant has her eggs and the cock leaves her for new fancy in his harem. Go near the nest and she will desert. How often will you find a nest of blue-stained, rotten eggs when the hay is cut down. Perhaps the country boy, on his journey with a ladle of oats to lure a pony off the hill, found the nest by accident, moved the grass, disturbed the place and made her forsake.

I remember finding such a nest. It was in the shelter of a gorse bush and when I found it the hen was sitting. She must have been paralysed in broody fever as some birds seem to be, for she did not rise. I could not resist touching

her. I stroked the wonderful smoothness of her back and hastened to bring my grandmother to see what I had found. I was thoroughly scolded for interfering with the hen, but two days later I crept back. The nest was there and the eggs too, every one as cold as the stones which lay about.

There was a time when the keeper would pay for information as to the whereabouts of pheasant nests. Make a journey to his cottage and he would give a shilling when he had confirmed the information. Usually the country lad would milk the nest of three or four eggs before telling the keeper. Once I met a bird-nester who carried a great pan-basket filled with the eggs of partridge and pheasant. I wonder now whether he knew the old way of testing an egg by seeing whether it would sink or swim, and knowing that if it sank it was not addled.

The Day of Butcher Murphy

BUTCHER MURPHY belonged to my father's day, and the day of my grandfather. Everyone to whom God grants three score years and ten must overlap an era, it seems. Were this not so there would have been no characters in my childhood, when, in fact, the ballad singer was still lingering and the last of the itinerants came to knock on the farmhouse door and play a tune for his 'piece', a soda scone and butter overspread with sweet gooseberry jam. The Butcher has gone, but his ghost, I am sure, still takes his place at the corner of the town square where he stood when I was a boy. There were no chromium plated cars in those days, no newly-rich tourists from Birmingham or Bermondsey searching for the remote to make it unremote, only the nags of the farmers standing with their heads down while they waited for their masters to finish their 'dram'. I cannot remember those ponies and gigs, the mongrel dogs in the gutter, the knot of youngsters before the red and yellow painted shop of the Italian ice-cream maker, without a vision of the Butcher too, no great landmark, an inconspicuous character, in fact. He was a noted poacher and I never heard of his being caught. His skill and cunning were well known. When he was missing, it was said that he had made an expedition after game. He always fired his shot from the road and concealed his gun in his clothes. When our trap turned into the main street, where we called on the saddler or the ironmonger, Butcher Murphy would give us good-day. His moustache straggled on his lip and added to his swarthy appearance. There was a glint in his eye, too, that made me consider him as an able man, one who could teach the rest a thing or two, one who knew more than he said.

I imagined, as I held the pony and waited until my grandfather had done his business with the merchant, that Butcher Murphy looked at the trees in the square, listened to the rooks quarrelling, and thought of a turn in the road where pheasants fed in the stubble or partridges went boldly up a stony brow, just clear of the hedge in his line of fire. When he bowed his head and spat between his boots he was thinking of the moves. The cart that was jolting along the road had swung slowly out of sight, the man 'looking' sheep had whistled in his dog and sunk behind the hill. The servant girl on her bicycle pushed self-consciously on her pedals and went round the bend, and Butcher Murphy took the gun out of his clothes and shortened barrels from his trouser-leg, the stock from the lining of his jacket and the fore-end from his pocket. Now the muffled click of the gun's assembling and the breach closing on the cartridges. One bright, sharp eye closing as the gun pointed at the feeding birds.

That corner was Butcher Murphy's corner. When I was

small he was there, and when I had almost grown to manhood he was still there, unchanged, for all I could notice.
The dog on the path before the Italian's ice-cream parlour
might be a different dog, but it was the same corner and
the same Butcher Murphy with his knowing look, a look
that appealed to my imagination and made me want to
know its secrets, a thing I never knew at first hand, though
gossip told enough to keep me for ever interested.

'Who was about town today?' they would ask at home.
'This one and that one, and Butcher Murphy on the
corner.'

It was when he was not there that his reputation was
made.

A while ago I met a man who had only poached once in
his life and his method was the strangest I have ever heard.
Owen drove a van for a country butcher in the days before
motor vans buzzed round the farms and villages. He was
sitting up behind his horse, letting the tired creature take
its time on a long hill when he saw ahead of him three
pheasants feeding on a bank above the road. There was
plenty of time to think. Owen looked for a weapon. There
was no loose stone by the roadside. He had no hidden gun,
but his eye caught his whip. At a distance of a few yards
from the feeding birds, he drew up the horse and stepped
quietly down on the grass verge. Somehow the movement of
a horse, or even a man on foot on a road, does not excite a
feeding bird or animal. Perhaps, like the crow pitching in
the wind on the top of a roadside elm, they know that the
stretch of road is a thing apart from the pasture and the
business of the man on the road differs from that of the
man on the field. Owen crawled up the bank without a

sound. The hen pheasant nearest to him jerked up her head in alarm and in that instant the whip cracked out and coiled itself about her neck and she scrambled and fluttered on the grass. The cock and the other hens burst into flight as Owen threw himself on to the top of the bank and grabbed the hen before she could become disentangled and take flight. The practised hand of the butcher's man quickly wrung her neck and, when the horse began its journey again and Owen leant forward on his seat to replace his whip, the pheasant lay behind him under the canvas.

Deer and Desperadoes

EVERY expedition in pursuit of game has something to mark it in memory: the rabbit that got away leaving only two tufts of hair to mark a near miss, the hailstorm that lashed the valley and made the leaves dance, the impudent fox that stood for a minute scratching itself before going through the hedge, the mixed bag in the snow when the woodcock, stockdove and widgeon kept company with the rabbit and the jack snipe. My first outing after a wild duck is a memory as vivid as any I possess. The rain had set in early in the afternoon, and a mist from the hills hung close above the fields. While I was crossing the farmyard three ducks came over low, flying one above the other. I stared at them, and as they vanished, I knew that they were off to feed in the waterholes of the moss. Hastening to the house, I rummaged in the drawer for four-shot cartridges, took down oilskins and lifted the gun. In half an hour I had crossed our march fence and was out across the moss, skirting the peat sloughs and the patches of green weed. No duck rose.

I went on and on with the light fading and the cry of high-flying curlews seeming muffled and far away. At length I came to more solid ground, a little hill with gorse dotted about and the paths of sheep criss-crossing it. I stopped. Right before me, no more than twelve feet from me, was the handsomest drake I had ever beheld. He was an immaculate bird of green, brown, fawn, blue, black and white. The drake feathers at his tail curled beautifully. The sheen on him could only have been painted. He stood,

his head raised, his eye bright and the white brands on his neck and wings showing. I caught my breath. There was an age that was yet no more than two deep sighs, and then he gave a quack and flapped into the air. I stood wondering whether I had seen a farmyard drake take flight or a mallard going off in search of a new and safer feeding ground. How easily I could have destroyed him and how hard it was to explain why I had not attempted to lift my already cocked gun!

Something of the same happened to me on the one and only occasion when a red deer was within range. I had strayed from the arable fields of an uncle's farm after three

hares that had frolicked through a little wood to the edge of
a drained bog. Losing the hares in tall grass and round
rushes that grew near a cluster of willows, I was walking
over the heaving bog towards more solid ground when a
young deer sprang out of the rushes into a small clearing
about ten yards ahead. I could not move. My hands and
arms stiffened and my heart bounded. The deer sniffed,
spun round on its back legs and sailed away, bound after
bound, into the brown and fawn wilderness, across the
peaty drain, through the willow boughs and into the deep
gloom of the thicket where the black earth oozed and
bubbled, where the tracks of moorhen feet showed on the
mud and lily leaves floated on pools. I recovered when the
deer had disappeared. I knew that it was useless to follow.
The bog would bear the weight of a fleeting deer, an
animal well used to the danger spots, but it was a death-
trap to a slow-moving man.

Although once in a year or two a farmer might find a
deer in his turnip field, the wind right, a gun in his hand
with the right shot in the cartridge, few deer were ever
killed on arable land. Here and there among the farmers,
nevertheless, a deerskin rug lay at a bedside. What better
place? Where could a man have such a rug that his visitors
might not see it, except in his bedroom? Poachers who
went after deer waited until the dry weather set in, when
the calf was in the willow thicket, lying among the rushes,
away in the silence of the waste. Those who had deerskin
rugs got them by sneaking in after the calf. The hind would
be off, but the calf, helpless little creature, would lie there,
twitching an eye as a fly ran over its face, moving its ears
anxiously as the prowler with the gun came near. My only

glimpses of deer from the 'forest moor' were when they dashed away over the hill, leaving a ravaged turnip field.

The law has been slow to take account of the deer poacher whose existence is entirely due to social change. The deer poacher a hundred years ago was hardly a poacher at all. He took no great toll of deer. Venison is strong and stringy meat and the demand for it was limited. The modern deer poacher came into his own after the Second World War. He was activated by the ruthless law of supply and demand. He set out to slaughter deer, delighted to get away with two if he maimed a dozen, prepared to shoot at anything that moved in the headlights of his van, whether it be a frightened buck or a foolhardy hill farmer. The automatic weapon taught some men how to kill. Guns that sprayed lead and killed at close range could be used on deer that came out of the mountains to search for food as the cold breath of winter spread in the uplands. Deer poaching became an organised business and the outcry against it came more from humanitarians than outraged feudal lords, for to tell the truth there were deer in plenty and no one's day's stalking was much imperilled by the deer poacher's activity. It is a sad truth that at this moment poachers make long journeys north to kill deer and bring their bag back to unscrupulous dealers. The times are in favour of gang activity on mountain and river alike. There is no hunting craft in what these blackguards do with soft-nosed bullets or spear and net. They would be content to mutilate a score of deer if they could achieve their end, let the dead fish float down in a dozen pools if they could fill their sacks and get away. The deer poacher was known in Norman times and was put to death if caught with royal

game, maimed and enslaved on suspicion of trespassing in
the chase. He was a bold man who killed a deer to feed his
family or earn himself a silver piece in days more enlight-
ened than those of Rufus, but the word poacher is too good
for the breed that slaughters the deer today. It cannot at
once be applied to men who had skill and cunning in the
ways of the wild, even whose secrets came from generations
of hunters as well as to the barbarian whose greed shortcuts
all human decency.

The Ways of the Fowler

GOING after wild duck I have often spent a long time in very cold water, hiding from the keeper, taking shelter in breast-high rushes and ducking when any wild birds flew over in case the sudden turn of their flight would betray me. Taking a shot at widgeon, I brought one down out in bog where floating islands of reeds drifted and the water flowed through all the growing vegetation, carrying the smallest fragments of green life in its stream. The widgeon fluttered and flapped beyond easy reach. I hated to see it flap away to die slowly and I had no dog. Risking the keeper's eye, I waded out. The widgeon flapped through the rushes. I strode forward. The water rose from my knees to my thighs and then chilled my stomach and waist. Perhaps the widgeon had lured me so that the bog could suck me down, for, when I suddenly became aware of the danger, it stopped flapping, began to swim forward, weaving through the dead wood and water-carried green stuff. The way back taxed my strength and it seemed for a while that the water did not become gradually shallow, although I had not noticed its sudden deepening on my way out. I had hardly got my water-logged boots on hard ground before the keeper clambered over a wall a hundred yards away and I had to run.

In Wales I was in the company of a local preacher when we crossed a farm, to the annoyance of the owner, who waved his stick and urged two sharp-nosed collie dogs after us. Later that day we returned across the same ground, jumping a stream on the way. My companion drew back. I thought he had spotted the owner waiting for us, but, as he held my arm, five or six fat ducks swam round a bend. Up went his gun. Two of the domestic ducks toppled in the water and the rest flapped into the hazels beside the stream. I laughed as he lifted his kill and we hurried on. I remembered my first mallard, and how easily it had escaped me.

Come across the moss after the grouse, the richly coloured red grouse that warns you from the heather shoulder to 'goback, goback, goback!' or the black grouse, with his forked tail, so black that he has a tinge of blue about him and little contrasts, the blood-red mark at his eye and the white beneath his tail. Out over the moss, on the edge of the peat hole, the crowing black cock will stop suddenly as he sees you. There they go, their wings a uniform down-curve as they skim the heather. There seemed to be no breeze, no chance of the birds rising from the ling where they were feeding, and now they have gone. Walk after them and as soon as you appear on a new skyline you will see them again in flight, off into the endless moss with its bog holes and black-faced, lonely-looking sheep.

Francie McGinn would breast the wind, his clothing moulded to his sturdy frame, his dog at his heels the whole time. Let the rabbit go, the odd rabbit of the moss, or the hare that slept out there on the little hill of sun-scorched grass: let them go, Francie would advise. Somehow his winding course over the drier ground would bring him to the layers of the peat cutting. The black cock's startling flight would not spoil his aim and his second shot would be directed at one of the great pack of grouse rising at the crash of the gun.

When you have done this once or twice, perhaps in the morning, or the afternoon when the sun lies low over the heather, you will learn how wary a bird is the black cock and how he sometimes perches in the old thorn tree. Take the bird home and let it hang, for even when it is ready for the pot it will be tough unless it is well cooked. There will be something of the flavour of the moss about him, the strong flavour of the heather roots. There will be the flavour of adventure, too, for out there on the open moor you were as conspicuous as the dead tree and the cairn.

When I think of the wild goose I remember a clear cold morning in late October. I was standing on a hill where I had set snares the previous day, and gazing across the farm-land at the strips of ploughing, the carpet squares of old pasture, stubble going grey, broken and patchy rows of turnips that reminded me of the havoc of the rooks after wireworm in early summer. All at once, in the fields below, the geese thrust up their necks and began to cackle. I could hear the sound faintly and was puzzled for a little while, and then I saw the long formations of the grey lag or pink-footed geese, I could not tell which they were. They came out of the hard sky of the north, no more than dots in V formation. In a little while I heard what the domestic geese had heard, the honking of the wild birds. They came on, high above the hill, and then wheeled, taking direction

from their leader and moving with a wonderful co-ordina-
tion and precision, to fly towards the great sand flats of
the estuary. Long after they were gone the farmyard geese
called. There was something pathetic in the call of the
heavy, earthbound birds.

Characters about the town would slip off just before
dusk, carrying a variety of ancient guns and hoping to
get one shot, or perhaps two, at the wariest of all birds, the
wild goose. It was a vigil depending on the wind, the moon
climbing at the back of of the hill, the glitter of the wet
sand and the run of the tide. The man who stood freezing
in the cutting wind might see no more than a formation
moving against a twilight sky, hear no more than the tink-
ling notes of the sand birds, the golden plover, the sand-
pipers, the dunlins, or the hoarse call of a stray wild
duck.

Once I took a trip up a river at dusk, watched most of
the way by a jealous keeper who hoped to catch me above
the high-water mark. The teal and widgeon, rose well
ahead of me and escaped. The sheldrake, that wonderfully
coloured duck that nests in the rabbit hole, and is so salty
and fish-flavoured that no one will eat it. evaded me with
care that was unnnecessary, and when I rounded a bend I
came upon a man in a punt with a great cannon clamped
in it.

'Look what you've done!' he bawled and rose from the
concealment of the rushes as dozens of water birds took
wing.

He had been lying there for a long time waiting for
enough of the poor creatures to come within range of
slaughter. Not long after this I read of a claim of a record

number of ducks being killed with one shot and I wondered how many more had been killed without being
recovered, for a wounded duck often dives and stays below,
holding fast to a reed or water weed until it dies.

Duck Catching

THE ways of taking a duck are limited by the habits of the bird and there are fewer poachers of waterfowl, but I remember reading a book that gave some account of the cunning of a north country poacher who had discovered how to catch duck, domestic or wild, without much fear of detection. This observant individual discovered that a number of posts had been driven into the bed of the river for some purpose. The tops of the posts were perhaps a foot below the river's normal level. He baited these places with succulent morsels beloved of ducks, putting his bait on hooks with short cords fastened to stones perhaps a third the weight of a duck. The duck would pick up the titbit, tug at it when the hook set, the stone would lift from the top of the post and slip into the deeper water taking the duck down with it. At night the poacher would row out and grapple for the birds at the bottom of the posts, finding each one within a small radius of the place where it had been caught. Such a method might have been devised by a fisherman rather than a fowler, perhaps.

Altogether, wild duck are not so well preserved. It cannot be denied that they are fostered and encouraged to breed. They are fed on jealously-guarded duck lakes. The flesh of the wild duck is not to everyone's taste. Its feeding habits make this so. An estuary duck may be muddy and salty in flavour. Its flesh is dark and not many people like it. There is no great profit to be had in bringing a sack of mallard and widgeon to the dealer's back door. The man who goes after duck does it for the love of hunting, just as most poachers shoot a woodcock and put his wing-tip feathers in their caps because the shooting of a woodcock takes skill with a gun. The poacher may be mooching through the wood, looking for a pheasant or letting his dog mark the undergrowth, when the woodcock rises from the mat of dead leaves. Every time a woodcock flies into a wood or out of it, his line of flight is the same, he will swerve past a particular tree and tower out over the tops of others in the same route without variation, but his flight is twisted, rapid wing-beats and a turn. Some of the poachers have a little rhyme they recite, like 'Polly put the kettle on', and at the last word the woodcock will twist so that, as soon as he has twisted, he is sighted with the swinging gun and the shot is fired. One winter, in the course of poaching expeditions, I collected sixteen wing-tip feathers and never once had I gone in search of a woodcock. An old man told me that in his youth artists would pay well for these stiff-quilled soft little feathers. I imagine that if they were of use, the artist was asked a good price for them, for there are only two of these feathers to a bird.

Perhaps of all the things in poaching that thrills a man, the narrow escape lives longest in his memory. Once I took hasty refuge in a ditch, where I lay, half covered by a low bridge and an overhanging bush. The farmer, who had

THE NEW POACHER'S HANDBOOK

called out his labourers to catch me, came and stood on the
bridge. I could have touched his boot, and lay in my uncomfortable shelter with a fast-beating heart. The noise of
the search died away and it seemed safe to come out, when,
for the first time, I realised that I had been under observation throughout the affair. A soldier and a girl had been
embracing in the grass on the other side of the ditch. Evi-
dently they thought I was a desperate character, for when I
came out, the girl caught nervously at her companion's
arm. I looked fiercely at them in case they decided to begin
shouting, and made long and fast strides to the nearest
cover.

Little Hugh told me that he once took shelter with a
companion, lying in the heart of a blackberry tangle. They
had been there five minutes when a black spaniel came
through the bush and began licking the face of Little
Hugh's companion. The man whispered that he had
brought an aniseed rag with him so that he could throw it
down to distract any dog sent after him! Little Hugh stood
up, risking discovery, and taking the rag, threw it with all
his strength across the wood, but the spaniel remained
until whistled for by its master and it was only by luck that
the pair escaped capture!

Lying in shelter, perhaps with head buried in the forest
of grass at the hedge bottom, the poacher learns how blind
a man can be and how much human sight and real observation depends on movement. If you get out of bed and join
the wild characters with the net and the gun you will learn
all these things: how to come by the rabbit, the hare, the
pheasant, the partridge and, perhaps, a fine or a week or
two in prison! The lessons of Black Bill, Little Hugh and

Francie McGinn are lessons in nature and the thing is dormant in all of us.

I have got you into bad company and infected you, perhaps, with a restlessness that will take you when your train carries you through wooded country, with the close-growing firs a yard or two from the line, when you catch a glimpse of a bouncing white tail, a countryman plodding over a field in the autumn daybreak. It is not my intention to incite you to get yourself into trouble.

The Quiet River

PUT away the gun, the ferret and the dog. Have done with such things. Let me take you to the singing water of the stream, to the deep heavy flow of the river, to study the ripple of the rising trout and hear the plop of the vole launching himself from the bank. Watch the speeding driftwood and the creamy scum that gathers where the trailing thorn rakes the current. In the quietness of the river's course you will come upon the moorhen travelling among the roots of the trees, for ever in search of something, in and out along the bank, through the grass and across the stones. You will come to the broken water over the rocks where the current swirls and bubbles, and here you will see the black and white dipper commit what seems to be suicide by wading into the depths of the flowing water. Up in the water-smoothed rocks you will catch your first glimpse of the salmon, going on, like a ploughing liner, to the sweeter water at the river's source, you will see the hovering trout or the spurt of gravel where he hovered until you moved. There are secrets in the taking of a fish, secrets known to the boy and the man from the cottage up the road, ways handed down to sons and to the sons of sons.

Put away the gun and taste the brown trout, the silvered sea-trout, the great salmon.

There is a time when summer is young and the wagtails are nesting by the water, when the flow of the stream slackens and the rocks begin to show. The pools here and there become shallow and the sound of the water dies and the man after a fish forgets how it frothed in colour when the spate of spring roared through the hollows and licked at the top of the bridge's arc. When the water only whispers and sighs and bubbles among the stones the boy from the cottage will come and lie on his stomach and watch the trout. In a little while he will begin dabbling his arms in the water, having dragged his sleeves almost up to his shoulders.

Watch him. He is at the old game of tickling a trout. His hands go feeling in under the belly of the rock. He knows the places where the biggest trout shelter. If you learn to tickle trout you will learn to move your hands in the way you reach for a ferret, without an excited, jerky movement. Smoothly, confidently. The trout, speckled brown and with a cream shade on its under-side almost a match for the delicate old tea rose, will remain motionless, or almost motionless: a gentle movement of the gills and the slightest balancing against the cold water coming down from the hills. At the coming of the searching fingers he will edge forward a fraction, aware, a little uneasy perhaps, but sure in his knowledge that one movement of his tail and fins and he will be off through the pool as fast as the brief reflection of the flying swallow. The hands of the boy are guided by his eyes. He lies sprawled over the rock. One violent motion and he might find himself head first in the pool, but the fingers spread and draw close to the trout. The fish floats higher, closer to the rock. Now the fingers gently reach the under-side of the fish and caress the slipperiness. The trout backs a little. The fingers stroke again and the trout edges back, nervously now, ready to dart away, and the boy waits his time. Now the trout has retreated until the gills are above the fingers and the hands take sudden hold in the only spot a hand can grip and retain a living fish in water. Now the trout is up in the air and its life going in fast gulps and a frantic jerking of its tail.

This is the way of tickling trout. Before you become a hand at it you will have many a wetting and lose a dozen or so, but the ragged boy from the village school would make a fine teacher.

Sometimes the tickling of a trout does not end by the method of snatching. The boy or man feeling the trout will have a kitchen fork in one hand, and when the tail of the fish is within stabbing distance will thrust the fork into it and hoist the trout out of the water. I remember watching boys from the country school tickling trout when the water was low, and they caught two or three fine fish while I stood by. Fish, I was told, that had grown old and cunning, disdaining the maggot, the fly and the worm.

The blacksmith, who could hardly keep his tools in his hands on certain days when the trout were in the pool below the bridge, often went angling. When he deserted the smithy he would leave a note on the door for any farmer who called. It would state briefly, 'Up the water' or 'Down the water', and the caller would either go away or go up or down the water to find the smith. I remember

calling with a mare than needed a set of shoes, and at the
moment of my arrival the smith was padlocking his door.
I tied the mare to a ring in the wall and went to him. He
was going fishing, he informed me. He had a hammer in
his hand and I could see no sign of a rod, or even a piece
of brown line. I followed him a yard or two to the bank,
where he sat down and took off his boots and socks and
turned up the bottoms of his trousers.

'Come on,' he said. 'You might as well, The mare'll not be
shod till I've done.'

He had stopped the water with a dam, he told me, and
now he was going fishing with a big hammer. Obediently,
for I could be persuaded to any such pastime with a glance
of invitation, I took off my boots and socks and waded into
the stream after the smith, gasping at the coldness of the
water and making grimaces of pain as I trod on a stone not
so smooth as it might have been. We came to the first pool.
The smith signalled to me and I stood down-water from
him as he indicated. He swung the heavy hammer above
his head. The sinews of his wrists rose and the hammer
came down with a great crash on the nearest rock. I caught
my breath, for a moment later a stunned fish floated out.

'Grab it!' yelled the smith.

I grabbed and managed to get it. We waded a few paces
and he struck another rock, but no trout had sheltered beneath. We moved again and he struck another without
result. All at once he stopped.

'Hell,' he said, 'look yonder!'

His landlord, carrying basket and rod, was coming up
the bank. We scampered to our boots. The smith lifted his
and ran over the cinders to unlock the smithy door. With

the fish in my pocket, and my boots untied on my feet, I hurried after him and led the mare in to be shod. He had put on his boots and was pulling at the handle of the bellows.

'If he shows face in the door,' he cursed, 'I'll put a hot iron on him!'

The owner of the smithy and the stream went past and the mare was shod. I promised myself I would get down to 'fish' with the smith again, but somehow the opportunity never arose.

Away in the quietness of the remote countryside there are streams where the trout are large, and safe, too, because the the banks are lined with thorn and briar and gorse and straggling patches of round rushes. Here the fisherman cannot come, for the stream winds and twists like a moving snake. In such a place I learned the art of setting lines.

Line Setting

WE had a ploughman working for us at that time, who lived
in the loft above the kitchen. He slept there, clattering up
the shaky wooden ladder after his supper to have a couple
of draws on a cigarette butt before resting at night, clattering down in the early morning to go off before his breakfast to feed and water his horses. He asked me to come to
his home with him on Sunday and spend the day wandering
the rough land looking for the eggs of peewit and curlew.
I had to have permission to go and I had not dared to ask
up to the moment on Sunday morning after breakfast when
the ploughman was washing himself at the pump. I
watched him preparing himself, scrubbing his rough red
hands, polishing his cramping Sunday shoes, wetting his
hair and combing it down. He went up the ladder, winking
at me, and I heard the sound of paper being wrapped
round his bundle of washing. I screwed up my courage and
asked while my grandfather was engrossed in Saturday's
paper, and could hardly restrain myself when told I might
go.

The ploughman's family were crofters. They ploughed
and harrowed two or three acres of light stony soil away in

a wilderness of round rushes, cotton grass and thorny thickets. Through this country ran the stream. Somehow the journey took away my eagerness to hunt for plovers' nests and cross swampy ground after the eggs of the moor-hen. The ploughman's brother was on his way down to the stream to look his lines, and I went with him. Along the winding stream he had set two or three dozen. He looked round carefully before going to them, for, remote as this place was, the water was 'owned'. Can a man own the clouds, the rain, the streams that trickle over the rocks? Can he own what the heron takes from the pool without permission, what the otter carries in his whiskered mouth? This water belonged to the owner of the land, however.

We walked the course of the stream. Half a dozen had 'taken' and I could see the trout drifting at the extremity of the line. They were fine fish. This was the way to catch the really big fish, I was told. The greedy little trout was in faster water. Here each big fish had a pool or a deep stretch at a bend all to himself. Even with a rod and the right bait, such a fish was hard to catch, and all the patience a man had could be easily exhausted dangling a line. The thing to do was to put down the right worm, a red-streaked worm from the midden, one with an irresistible flavour. The trout would not look at it in the first hour. The slab of stone where the fine sandy gravel tumbled along in the current screened him from the fishing heron. His appetite was delicate. Only in the hours of darkness, perhaps the hour before dawn, would this big old trout venture to feed. He might contemplate the worm with midden flavour for a long time before he took it, but in the end he would bite. His struggles might fray the gut before the hook, but in the end he would give up. Perhaps in the cold air of the morning he would stiffen and float, or perhaps he would sink sadly down to the side of the stone and wait to be lifted out with no fight left in him.

First go to the midden's edge and dig for the red-marked, thin little worm. Gather the bog moss from a waterhole and let the worms cleanse themselves in it for a day or two. Cut pegs like those for snares and tie a couple of yards of brown line to each peg and a hook to each line. Make sure the pegs have been soil-stained or the warden will spot them. When they are ready, fill the pockets of your coat with the lines and set out for the chosen stream. Here are the places. The water ceases to ripple and goes smooth over the pot-hole. Set one here. Drive the peg right into the bank. Drop the worm-baited hook into the water. Move on a few yards. The current sweeps round the bend and flows away in under the overhanging bush. Put another in the bank here and let the bait be swept in under the bush. Walk on to the big stone. The water runs right underneath part of it, and up in the dark cold tunnel the big old fish soberly takes the water of the springs in through his mouth and lets it out through his gills. Let the line snake from the bank out over the stone so that the worm is at the entrance to the cavern. In time he may be tempted.

You must study this art. Someone else may be setting the water at the same time, someone with no more conscience than yourself. He may have an alarm ringing in his cottage half an hour earlier than yours, and when he comes down the water having an eye for all things natural and unnatural, he may spot your setting places. Where the stream has bare, stony banks, reach into the water, and lift out a big stone. Tie the brown line to this stone and put it back in the water. Leave a little indicator of some kind to remind you of the place, one stone perched on another, or a piece of dead wood among the shingle. Where the bank is fringed with undergrowth, let the line go down a branch that trails in the current. Where trees overhang, let the line drop from a low branch. On each line, close to the hook, tie a fair-sized stone, so that the hooked fish will not float to the surface and so betray the fact that lines are being set.

I can remember making long journeys at daybreak to look carefully set lines, and, making the first journey along the water I have often failed to spot my own lines. Having found the first of them, however, I usually come on the others with little difficulty. Once I arrived to disturb a heron that rose quickly and crashed at once because he had my hooked fish in his mouth and, retaining his hold on it, he rose a foot or two and was dragged out of the air. He quickly abandoned the fish and flapped off with a cry of annoyance.

The setting of lines is only one of the ways in which a poacher comes by a trout. There are many ways, and for one of them at least he will make a dam. The making of a dam is a thing for which it is best to have assistance. Put on some long boots and wade into the stream. Move the stones until they form a barrier. Add a turf or two to plug the holes, and gradually build higher until the flow is reduced to a trickle. It is a thing best done in the dry spell of early summer. When the flow is stemmed, the pools are no more than puddles and the stranded fish can be grappled for with the hands.

Two men of the village regularly sneaked off on a quiet summer's night to dam the stream, empty the pools and clear a stretch of the stream's course of big boulders so that it would be ready for netting in a week or two. The netting of a stream is a furtive process, sometimes carried out when the boys of the village are posted to watch. The net is taken by one of the poachers, who wades the water at a shallow place and sets off up the other bank, drawing to the first shallow, where the bottom is drawn in advance of the top, the catch bagged in the net and lifted clear of the stream.

Otters and Otter Boards

Two kinds of otter are known to the devotees of trout fishing. The otter that swims through the pool and the otter that is made to swim through it, or across the quiet mountain lake. An otter board is a sizeable piece of wood roughly shaped like a keel. On one edge it is weighted with lead. The lead keeps most of the wood well below the surface of the water. Rigged from the flat side of the board are three cords that terminate in a line, the whole thing looking very much like the rigging of a kite. In fact, the object is to make the wooden kite sail into the current as a paper kite sails aloft. The line, paid out by the poacher, is festooned with 'droppers'– a length of nylon (it used to be gut in the old days) to which is attached a sizeable trout fly. The effect of the board being drifted and undulated by the current of the river or the lake (the wind being the governing factor in this case) is to make the string of flies work in an attractive fashion. When the otter is worked by night, when big fish are feeding, the first fish that takes imparts movement to the whole line and makes all the flies jig and dance. The more fish that take the better the otter works and the better the poacher likes it. Ottering on mountain lakes is mainly done by night not only because the bigger lake trout remain inactive until after dark but because the otter men work in comparative peace, one operating the board and his companion sitting on a high rock to listen and watch for the approach of the keepers.

It is a rather sad fact that when a lake has been ottered a few times the fish become 'hook-shy' and no longer rise freely to the fly, but it remains, in spite of everything, one of the most popular ways of taking trout from remote lakes in Wales and I have no doubt that poachers in England, Scotland and Ireland are no less skilled in the use of the board. One of the most audacious otter board poachers I have heard of was a man who was caught on a lake not far from where I live now. He had been seen sailing a model yacht for many days, playing, it seemed, like a child until it was discovered that he had a 'string' to his boat and the little sailing boat was in fact carrying a set of flies over the trout. The keepers who had no time for model yachts and such childish pastimes, hauled the gentleman off to court and taught him that three flies at a time are as much as any man need fish.

I had been keeping company with a Welsh poacher for a long time before he disclosed that he possessed a snatching hook, a gaff or cleek, as it is called elsewhere. One day, when he was showing me an old muzzle-loading gun he had inherited from his father, who had started life, like many another country boy in the old days, as a scarecrow, he looked around carefully and said, 'Ever seen a snatching hook?' Like the old gun, he had had it from his father, who had had it from his own father. I felt, by the caution he displayed before mentioning the subject, that we had reached a rare intimacy. I looked at the hook. It was old and rusty. Many a fine salmon had been lifted with this hook, he whispered. Away where the river forked and came down in mare's-tails from the rocks of the hills and, long ago, when a day's travel had been as far as a horse could run or a man could walk, his forebears had hung about the lonely places when the salmon was running upstream to spawn. He explained how it was used. I listened, not because I had not seen one before, but because it confirmed my belief that these things were shared and had been shared by all country folk from the beginning.

The hook is four or five inches in length. It has a shank which is hollow. The point may be barbed or it may not. In the shank there is a hole through which a strong rope is tied and the strands of the rope are bound down neatly. The rope may be five or six feet long and at its end is a loop through which a man can put his hand. The gaff is not a gaff until the poacher cuts himself a stick. As a rule the stick could be mistaken for a walking stick, a hazel rod such as any idling countryman might have in his hand when walking by the river.

Out in the deep current the salmon are crowding. The fresh current, filled with the intoxicating oxygen, the flavour of the higher land, prompts one of them to plough into the shallower water, navigate the pools and come to the fall, the place where the river breaks and tumbles over the rocks. Now the fine fish lashes its tail and throws itself at the torrent. The leap fails and it drifts back. The man among the small stones and shingle plays with his stick. The salmon tries again and again. Now it floats back exhausted and lies in a near-at-hand pool recovering its strength, silvered and magnificent, a thing to take the breath away, The man by the water fumbles in his pocket, draws out the hook, drives his stick into the socket, pulls the rope tight so that all is firm, and looks round. In that instant he makes up his mind. The cold mountain water may swirl round his boot heads, but he will not feel its icy bite. The rod and the hook will reach out suddenly and the salmon will thresh the waters as it slashes into its side. For perhaps three minutes the tug-of-war will go on. The hazel rod, no longer needed, will swim dizzily round the next pool and then come aground on the rocks. The salmon, hauled to the side and cracked on the head, will cease to struggle, and the poacher will scramble to the nearest cover to hide it or pop it into his sack.

There is such an air of innocence about the snatcher. He smokes a pipe and stares at the pools, the dark water, glinting with the glimmer of light that penetrates the screen of the overhanging fir. In Wales he might be mistaken for a rustic poet. Down the water, perched on a crag, his young son keeps watch. The fish is sold before it is caught. The hotel up the valley will hand over money at the back door. What angler could guarantee a fish for the dinner table on Sunday night?

Once I went fishing in a river, playing for a trout with a dry fly or some such lure. I stood a long time casting over a pool below a weir, sharing the water with an old man who ran out of patience too. He reeled in his line and grunted his disgust. A salmon came through the pool, making a wash like a liner. The old man suggested we went elsewhere, pointing to a small boy who played near the weir. It seemed the boy had a snatching hook and was waiting for us to go, so that we might not witness the offence. His mother kept watch from a vantage above the weir. We found a new pool and began casting once more. My companion tired quickly and soon left me. Curious, I went down the bank after him. I could not get near enough to find out, but I was sure he was bargaining with the mother of the salmon snatcher!

Snatchers at Work

TIME can't be halted to please any of us. It is an often re-
peated truth that we never look at the same river again.
Day after day more people come to the river to fish, old
hands bringing apprentices, ignorant enthusiasts elbowing
their way in and suffering the frustration that lack of knowledge and skill must invariably bring, for the fact that there
are fish in our rivers at all proves that survival depends on
fish and fowl becoming conditioned to danger and the ways
of predators of all kinds. The newcomers to the salmon
pools cannot always use a gaff. The pools are often deep and
the salmon lie down there out of danger. To catch them
some ingenuity is required, ingenuity and the benefit of
science in some cases. Simple salmon snatching is done by
men who are also anglers of considerable skill. They are
poachers who are masters of the art, for they can snatch their
salmon with a worm on their hook without seeing the fish,
but knowing the river so well that even where the water is
churned in a gut beyond a weir they can tell within inches
where a salmon rests at anchor. Two or three casts and
they have hooked their fish, and, one might admit, earned
their reward by cunning and guile.

The less skilled salmon snatcher puts a trailing hook on his salmon fly, knowing that salmon will often rise to follow a fly without snatching at it or attempting to take. Jerking the fly through the water the snatcher can hope that it will at some time or other swing the trailing hook into the side of the curious salmon. It requires a certain speed when the fish is brought to the bank to ensure that the trailing hook is cut off and the wounded fish made to look simply as though it had been gaffed, inexpertly gaffed, perhaps, if the snatcher's hook took it in an unlikely place. Two other ways make the 'art' of snatching less of a gamble. Both are so widely known that I hardly think I do much harm to speak of them. A man may wear polarising glasses in order to see his fish the better (I hardly ever see an angler wearing these things without I wonder about his ethics) or dress his hook in a way that he can see it in comparatively deep but clear water. In one part of Wales they used a shirt button, a small pearl button and a treble hook. The button would be fastened to the line a little way from the hook and the angler, when he made his cast, would keep his eyes skinned for a sight of the button, a small white spot drifting down the pool, marking the whereabouts of the treble hook. When the hook and the button crossed or passed under a 'hovering' salmon they would be allowed to drift only the distance necessary to allow for the current and the refraction of light. This having been allowed for, the rod would be smartly lifted and the hook driven into the fish.

Even a small thing like a shirt button excites suspicion. A keeper seeing it might pause long enough to consider whether or not the angler was up to some crime or other. The really cunning poacher soon thought up a refinement, putting on a scantily dressed fly with a large hook and using a marker in the shape of a leaf with a silver underside. Hitching the leaf to the cast is no problem and a leaf passing downstream is harmless enough. Even the salmon is used to that, but the marker is there and the snatcher needs no more to guide his hand.

The man with glasses need not, of course, go quite so far where the rules allow him to fish prawn or shrimp, things easily seen, or where he is allowed to spin a Silver Devon. He may trail this bait or spinner in the current, waiting for the fish to advance to make its jump. Salmon ascending a river seem to inspect even minor falls before they make their leap, having a built-in mechanism that lets them know how high the rocks above water are, perhaps. As the fish comes forward and rises the prawn or shrimp swings in the current something like the swinging of a trailing weed. At the right moment the angler who can see into the pool even in brilliant sunlight because he is wearing glasses for that purpose gives a twitch to his rod and the line is sent in a new arc which, if he is lucky, drives the hook into the side of the fish. He can do this as often as the fish comes up to judge the falls which, on warm days and when water is low, may be many times. One salmon in a day isn't bad even for a snatcher.

Less refined is the method newly come to the river with the advent of the aqua lung, frogman's gear and underwater spear-guns. Already poachers have been 'taken' from pools garbed in flippers and goggles. Salmon are not always able to escape down river. Indeed as every salmon angler knows, many a fish is locked in a particular pool for weeks in summer, growing redder than the choicest middle cut ever advertised. The bold swimmer may get into the water and chase his salmon until he catches it. The flippers protect his feet from the sharp rocks, the goggles enable him to see what he is doing and all he needs is the knowledge that the gills are the only sure hold a man can get on a living fish. If he has a spear he can spear his salmon. If he carries a gun he can shoot it. He relies on one thing, however, the remoteness of the pool from roads and bridges and the infrequency of the visits of keepers and owners. It is a dangerous business, without doubt, and spear-gun poachers have been known to have accidents brought about by their own over-enthusiasm for entering pools from which it was difficult to escape against the flow of the current.

A Noose for Trout

NOT every fish that is taken from a river is snatched or speared. Nor could one lump these with the rest taken by legal means and say that the ways of taking fish are limited to hook and barb.

Where the high arc of the bridge crosses the stream a boy lies over a slab of stone, gazing, it seems, at his own reflection in the water beneath, his arms immersed to the elbow in the current, the sleeve of his ragged jersey mopping moisture unheeded. In his hands he has a noose of brass wire, a strand unravelled from a rabbit snare, straightened and remade into a new snare, a snare for a trout. Here is the skill of the greatest of anglers. He moves the snare through the water, gently, slowly, a fraction at a time, and as the noose advances the trout retreats, going back, back into the safety of the hole below the slab of stone. The boy leans out, his hair brushes the water. His eyes see only the moss green and the red dots of the trout's back and flank, the yellow tinge of the water, the small, dark stones. Now the trout has touched the stone with his tail and edges forward again. The brass wire quivers in the force of water that sweeps round the cavity. The noose is about the trout. An age passes, an age in which the boy's ears pound with the sound of his own pulses, the background noise of the flowing water. The brass wire comes nearer and nearer the gills and when it is there the boy's hands draw on the noose and the fish is caught. This is the way of the 'girn' or snare, a way as skilful as tickling, as old as the spear.

The diligence of the village boy after the trout is a thing to be seen to be believed. His absorbed interest will keep him by the bank until his angry parents have become weary of calling. Without the snare or the toasting-fork spear, he will be cupping his hand to holes in the bank, careful to allow nothing to escape while he gently probes the depths of the hole with a withy wand. The probed trout will move uncomfortably and, when the stick is withdrawn, dart out to escape, and end in the grabbing hand of the boy. More than once the boy fishing in this way will find a cornered water-rat in his grasp and perhaps have his fingers nipped.

The water that ran through the quiet wood, over the stones and under the bridge, to froth and sing through the farms, is deserted by the heron and the signs of the otter are gone. Even the waterhen has deserted the banks. The fish are gone. There was a life about the place last year. It seemed that the sun kissed the water in the morning and gave it a sunset radiance before dusk. The eddies and the pools knew the motionless heron, stock-still in contemplation, the musical, stone-skipping wagtail and the life along the banks. The poachers who work on a large scale called in the half light of a summer's evening and caught all the fish; yes, like the Hamelin piper, they took every one! Up in the shallows they threw down a bag of lime and away down below the bridge they set a net across the water. Just before daylight, when all the water was discoloured, and every fish suffocated, they drew the net up. No fish escaped. The old brown trout that rose, nibbling at the drifting fly, the leaping, lively fish that threw himself in a fine curve into the sunlight, every fish from beneath the biggest and the smallest stones, every fish came up with the net, floated and drifted against it and ended in the poachers' basket. These are the townsmen who bring mass production methods with them. For them the way of line-setting is too slow.

Two or three poachers come out to the water and set a net. They have a van parked in the shelter of the trees. Perhaps they throw a bag of lime into the stream, perhaps they buy a tin of carbide and punch a few holes in its sides, for this method works well. Perhaps they are even more impatient and use a chemical that poisons fish as well as the stream, and let providence look after the man who eats the strangely flavoured trout or salmon! When they are about, the bailiff had better stay at home, or confine himself to the activities of the cottager, or he may finish the night crawling out of a pool like a half-drowned cat.

Where the lake or loch is in the bosom of the hills with only the shepherd's cottage in sight and the winding grey road close to the water, the 'aristocrat' of poachers will come in his car. Two or three of them will unload a canvas punt and some sticks or cans of fused explosive. The hills will echo with the detonations. The quiet waters of the loch will spout upwards and subside and the poachers will row out and gather the catch with nets and gaffs. Here they will take the big lake trout, leaving the shattered corpse of the pike or the perch.

The discovery of this method seems to have been made by soldiers who bombed the rivers of France in 1914–18. It is sometimes used by poachers who have tried for a long time time and without success. A fish lives in a deep pool and has scars of battle upon him, perhaps two or three flies and a worm hook in his lip. The men who know the pool have named this fish. Time has made a legend of him and the desire to hook and take him has grown hot and then changed to a desire to preserve him. Among the more desperate of the poachers is one who works in a quarry and can get hold of detonators, fuses and the like. He picks a day when the wind is high and his neighbours are about their firesides, and goes down to the pool with his cocoa tin, slow match and net.

When the men who know the pool next visit it they see the signs and know the old trout is gone. The round stones have been moved a little and a streak of colour comes from the gravel. They shake their heads and click their tongues, but they know that sooner or later this thing would have happened, even in the pool below the bridge, right in the middle of the village. There, at low water, a boy would have caught him with a snare or speared him with a fork. Perhaps he would have been caught in the shallows and stoned to death like many a fish venturing in dangerous water at a time of drought. The old trout will become a topic of conversation in the public-house for a while, and, when the thing is long enough forgotten, various braggarts will claim to have caught him with a worm or fly!

The Gorse Dam

THEY were never behind in their methods, the old poachers of Wales, although they never advertised their skill. Salmon have been coming up to spawn in the fresh, clear water of the mountain streams since the beginning of time. Once, legend says, everyone could catch the innocent salmon at his cottage door if a river or a stream was so close at hand. Once the salmon crowded the ditches and filled the feeders of the river and old ladies and small boys helped themselves. The poachers could not have been born then. They surely developed their art when things were harder come by and authority's hand became heavier. The salmon, however, still sought the ditches and nosed their way up the feeder streams as they do to this very day. In October the air of the hills is cool, the mists hang, the heather is dead and all the bloom gone from the gorse. A great rust spreads over the bracken slope and the raven and the carrion crow come back to the valley, for there is nothing left for them on the cold mountain. The valley farmer and the cottager sees the salmon in the peat-tinged water of the feeder. They are there, he tells himself, to be caught by him who has the cunning to catch them. He goes off upstream with his bill-hook or his hedging knife and begins to cut down the gorse bushes. When he has enough gorse he waits for the salmon to come up, and then, going below the spawning fish, fills the bed of the stream with gorse, making a dam which he tramples down until it is a thick and impenetrable barrier. This done, he shepherds the salmon down again, flailing the water with a stick. The frightened salmon bolts into the gorse barrier, driving into it until he can go no farther nor extricate himself if he wanted to. The farmer lifts his harvest and drags the gorse out of the stream.

This brings to mind another rather simple device used for catching big eels in lakes and ponds, although I doubt whether anyone can ever be said to have 'poached' an eel. The 'angler' gets himself a bale of hay or makes a truss of hay in the centre of which he plants a quantity of such offal as the entrails of a chicken or some larger creature. A rope is attached to the hay bale and it is cast out or lowered into the lake or dam. After a couple of days, the 'essence' of the hay having spread, eels will have discovered the treat and burrowed their way into the bale to gorge upon the offal. It is a simple matter to pull the rope, retrieve the bale and with it the feeding eels. The biggest freshwater eel I ever heard of was said to have been taken by this method. The skin of this eel was pinned to a stable door. It covered the door's length. The eel was said to have been thicker than a man's arm. Another vast eel was taken in a hay bale in another place twelve miles away and a bigger one got away to be trapped shortly afterwards in a water turbine.

Nets and Netsmen

MORE battles have taken place between netsmen and bailiffs as I have been writing, and I fear that the worst of all salmon poachers are those who run a net across the river after dark. Netting is a business for no less than two men. It generally involves a gang. When the gangs are disturbed the sort of war that once was waged between keepers and poachers on pheasant preserves breaks out anew. Today my newspaper carries the story of a netsman who went out to take salmon with other members of a gang and came not home with the break of day nor saw the sun rise again. Let me, however, talk of a modest salmon poacher.

Let me show you Snib, for I cannot undertake to introduce you. Snib is a close character. He hangs about the bridge until the public-house opens in the morning. He spits tobacco juice into the river while he waits for opening time in the evening. He has very little to say. When the cormorant bobs up and dives again he watches it with detached interest. Perhaps he is making an idle bet with himself as to where it will rise, or perhaps he is absorbed in scratching the hair below his cap. He completes the scene for the visitor. There is always a man looking at a river on a

sunny afternoon, watching the whorls of water, the fragments of vegetable and animal life that spin and glide
under the bridge and out towards the estuary. Snib makes
the scene complete, but he does not watch the water for the
bubbles and the whorls. He watches for the salmon coming
up. When the tide runs out he will take note of the
obstacles revealed at low water and when it is dark he will
remember.

Stand close to the bar and hear him whisper, 'A nice fish
for tomorrow?' When he speaks of fish he means only one
fish, the salmon. He and his son have a net and a boat and
no conscience or love for the bailiff. In the dark Snib will
remember what he saw in the afternoon, the tree branch
that had bedded itself in the sand below the bend, the
tangle of wire collecting weed and rubbish just at the bend.
He and his son will wrap rag round the oars, put the net
into the boat and paddle themselves down the water in a
darkness like the crow's wing. When they are past the bend,
the wire obstacle and the submerged tree, they will draw to
the bank, stake down the net and then row silently across
the water. Snib will feed out the net. The weighted side
will sink and the other will float, supported by the corks
along its edge. The running tide will belly the net, and the
salmon, swimming with the current, will come to the
meshes. In a little while, and without more than a whisper
between them, Snib and his son will row back, drawing
the net in a sweep to the other bank. Snib will step ashore
and his son will follow him, dropping anchor while he gives
a hand. The salmon will be big enough if they are eight to
twelve pounds in weight. One netting will be enough. It is
a dangerous game, for there is a regulation about a licence

and another about the size of the mesh of the net, as well as the number of fish that may be taken.

In the morning Snib will be at the kitchen door asking if he can have a word with the hotel keeper or his wife. Something about a salmon at twelve or thirteen shillings a pound and as fresh as the morning.

There is a way of getting salmon more often written about than used. The story books are full of daring characters who go to the river at night armed with lanterns and spears. Perhaps it happens, away in the steep banks where the river flows through the very heart of the hills, where the fir trees cling to the incline and a lantern could be hung above the water without attracting the attention of half the countryside. I know a blacksmith who made spears long ago, but he thought they were to be used for taking exhausted salmon from pools in daylight. I doubt whether an honest poacher would use such a risky method. It is like the legendary story of the irresistible salmon roe. A bit of salmon roe, they say, will get a salmon in water where no more than eels have been seen before! Where can I get the salmon roe? Who has this wonderful stuff? Perhaps it is kept with the supply of poles and lanterns that dot the course of rivers in the adventure stories of poaching. When the lantern is held over the water the salmon rises, fascinated by the light, and then the poacher thrusts with his spear. No doubt it works well enough, but the water bailiff, where is he? Hold on a minute. Make sure the indistinct form in the lantern's glow is not the reflection of the bailiff looking over the spearman's shoulder!

When you go to the trout water, or after the salmon in the river, you will have to know the bait to use. Go to the fisherman down the water and get a prawn for the salmon. The salmon, they say, does not fancy the fly, which merely irritates him, but he will snatch at the prawn. The cleansed worm will do for either trout or salmon when the colour of the spate is on the water. The boy who goes after pike will catch a bright green frog among the rushes, fasten it on his hook and let the frog struggle and flounder across the water. If he can find a mouse he will hook it well and throw it out into the deep stretch where the pike rests. The big fish, always ravenous, will seize it and swallow it in one move-ment. Shift the stones of the ditch, arrange and rearrange them until you isolate a little fish they call a bull-head. You will know him. He is no bigger than your thumb. Take him to the lake and hook him. The pike or the sharp-finned perch will speed for him and the line will be dragged into the depths.

The blacksmith I knew long ago would make himself a fly. Down by the water in the evening he would swipe at a live fly dancing above the stream and rescue it quickly be-fore it was carried away. With the small feather from a sparrow or a bantam, a little bit of coloured thread and perhaps a strand of hair, he would wind a fly on to a hook, as neat and smart a fly as the one that danced in the soft breeze of the evening. This fly would be the one the trout were taking, the one he could float on the smooth water in below the overhanging tree. It would set up a little ripple, no more than that caused by a thistledown moving on a still puddle, no more than a weary fly, turning round and round, right on the very surface of the water, somehow making it seem thick like rich cream. Down in the shadowed depth the trout would watch the fly, then rise to inspect it, let it pass and suddenly spin to snatch it down. The blacksmith would jerk the oiled line in his fingers and tighten, taking up the slack. By the time the trout was in his hand he would have the recovered line already wound round his cap and the home-made fly cut from the lip of the fish. He liked to fry them on a shovel above the fire in the forge and eat them with his fingers. They were tasty this way, he said. Small ones were cooked and eaten just as they came from the water, without gutting. A trout, he maintained, was a fastidious fish and took nothing that was not clean and delicate in flavour, but I could never share this theory or his appetite. I liked to see the fish dressed with a bit of fresh butter in the frying pan!

Sundry Adventures

CYCLING over the hills to a river that seemed as far away as ever, a friend and I came into a valley in which stood a fine old mansion surrounded by lawns and old elm trees. Before the main windows was a lake. We stood for a while, weary of the endless ride, watching the lake. It was exposed. There was little cover between the road where we stood and the edge of the lake, but as we took our breath we thought of big carp, or pike or perch, and in a little while it became impossible to go on in search of the river. Assemble the rods and make a hasty dash across the park to the shelter of the tall rushes in the hope that some part of the swampy bank would give us access to a fishing place. We made this plan, hid our bicycles and baited our hooks. It seemed we had not been noticed from the big windows of the mansion. We reached the rushes and found an opening. The lake here was shallow. The sunlight dappled the mud and weeds. While I stared, the biggest carp I had ever imagined swam majestically through the shallows. I cast my line. The blue clay worm wriggled on the surface of the mud. The carp came on, like a fat old gentleman promenading. He seemed to pass my worm and then all at once the line was tugged and a cloud of mud discoloured the shallows. The carp had gone and my big worm with him. I drew the line out of the water in disgust and at that moment a heron flapped out of the reeds a little way along

the bank. His flight was heavy and he alighted on the grass. I rushed at him waving my rod, and he rose and made off, leaving me a handsome perch which flopped and jumped among the grass and raised his stiff dorsal fin as I seized him. The stiff fin had forced the heron to come to earth

THE NEW POACHER'S HANDBOOK

in order to make an end of his victim, but I gave the perch a nice tap on the head and put him in my bag.

We moved gradually from tree to tree, from one patch of rushes to another, until we found deep water and could fish. The finest fish of the afternoon was the one the heron caught for me. We caught several perch, but the carp kept away. Perhaps they patrolled the shallows at the far end of the lake. Perhaps we lacked the paste bait or the chicken's guts that would have attracted them. In the late afternoon we discovered an old punt moored beneath a tree and pushed off in this hoping to get to better water. We were both fishing happily enough when we noticed a party strolling down the front lawn of the house. In our sudden panic our lines became entangled, the punt shipped several gallons of water and all our bait went overboard along with the punt-pole, so that we had to pole ourselves to the bank with the rods. The group on the lawn turned out to be several young men in the company of an elder man. They were coming to swim, it seemed.

I found myself on the bank, tearing at a tangle of lines and hooks and striving to get a rod to pieces, when the first of the party reached me.

'Now you've spoilt it!' I shouted angrily. 'If you are coming here to swim I'll have to go somewhere else!'

I could hardly believe my own ears. Their mouths fell open. I managed to get the tangle hacked apart and the rod taken down. With some of my longest strides I made off for the road, hurrying without too much loss of dignity, I hoped. In the village, several weeks after, I heard how some of the most impudent poachers ever had fished in the lake before the mansion, and I smiled. Legend had given us a

great bag of fish, put inches on our shoulders and a belli-
gerent air to our deportment. I remember well putting my
catch to wash in the kitchen sink and seeing most of the
perch, so tenacious of life, reviving and swimming around.

We went to a lake in the mountains a little later in the
summer. Here, we were told, there were big lake trout,
some almost as big as salmon and as old as the hills. We
hired a boat from a cottage near the lake and pushed off,
hopeful of a bag of lake trout. We had brought a can of
maggots, flies, worms and pickled minnows. After the first
few pulls on the oars the boat began to fill with water. A
wind came down from the mountains and a great black
cloud crawled over the lake and hung there, making the
water look like pitch. The wind carried us down the
lake. We had to row against the gale and bale feverishly.
Only once did a fish rise and the reel whined out with
neither of us able to do anything about it. The bait had
dangled on the water and annoyed a trout. When a breathing spell came and we were able to wind the line in again,
the hook and bait had gone. We brought the sinking boat
to the shore and made our way down the track to the
village, cured of a desire to catch the elusive lake trout and
concluding that our lack of success had been due to the fact
that we had lost our nerve and bought a licence to fish, even
if we had ignored the rule about using only a dry or wet fly!

An Eel from the Stream

MY interest in fishing began in an unorthodox manner.
Willie, who used to get all the odd jobs to do, often got
sent to the far end of the farm to clean ditches and streams.
He would labour there in the coolness of a hollow, clearing
the undergrowth, shovelling out the stones, the clumps of
sweet-smelling myrtle, the white-rooted cress and the garlic-
smelling weed and, as often as not, an eel or two. Some of
the eels he caught were more than two feet long. I can
remember how he would clamber out of the stream's bed
and search the bank for an eel, to chop its head off and
watch its decapitated body lashing frantically. Such eels, he
told me, would gash a man's palm if he dared grasp them.
As a consequence of this information I was always nervous
of a live eel and made a poor job of despatching it if I happened to get one on my line.

Occasionally, nearer home, where the stream widened its
banks and the farm ducks swam to and fro in a kind of drill,
a trout would show itself. The appearance of a trout in this
bit of water was a rare thing, for the ducks, aided by an odd
goose, seemed to take every weed and snail from the stream.
Even my set lines were a menace, for the greedy birds were

always in danger of getting themselves hooked. Here the water belonged to the rats that made their homes in the bare peaty banks and the arrogant ducks from the farmyard, until one evening I heard a disturbance down by the

water. The ducks were scattering and one drake was making a pathetic noise. I hurried to the stream. The other ducks, twitching their tails nervously and making small talk among themselves, waddled off up the field in a hurry. I found the drake. He was dying, huddled in by a tuft of grass on the bank. Blood streamed from his neck. I wondered about his death for a while until an otter was taken in a trap on another stream not so far away. Until this day, apart from one trapped specimen, I have seen no more of an otter than the wash of his snout as he crossed the river at dusk.

However few were the fish in this bit of water, which in places flowed out and deserved the name of stream, and in others narrowed and became a ditch, it began my interest in fishing. Here I cornered a minnow in my cupped palms, here I watched the snaking progress of the eel, marvelling at its gracefulness in the sun-heated water. In this place I stood and started at the waterhen taking flight with trailing feet, going hastily up to the narrows and making a little furrow in the slow current, a thing that spread out in delicate ripples and vanished before it lapped the banks. The biggest eel I ever saw moved in this stream. It came as I slumped over the wall gazing into the water, and it moved idly, waving its broad tail for all the world like the leaf of a submerged flag, except that it was brown and partly transparent, instead of opaque like the green leaf. I could have speared him with a fork, but I watched while he crossed the sun-kissed patch between a great slab of rock and a few round boulders. I was very small. It was a wonderful thing and thrilled me as only the lightning dart of a trout could thrill me after. I enjoyed the moment or two just as I later enjoyed the sight of the first brown trout I ever caught, marvelling at the beauty of its colouring, the marking of its dark back, so well matched to the bed of the stream, the shade of its under-side, cream, tea rose, honeysuckle, the shade of the belly of the stoat.

When I came to know the way of setting lines I wandered far afield to the streams that had fish in them. My aunts would sit in the early summer evenings, anxiously watching the clock and wondering if they dared tell my grandfather I was so late. Once, indeed, they made a search, imagining that they might find me head down in some deep pool, but I met them before they reached the water. I had a nice fish or two threaded on a piece of stick, but my catch went unnoticed while they foretold in angry relief the desperate end that would one day surely befall me if I persisted in such shiftless ways.

There was one place that tantalised me and attracted me to day-dream. It was a place we called the Cut, a deep gully blasted through the rock for the purpose of draining an old loch. The Cut was about fifteen to twenty feet deep and absolutely inaccessible. The water that ran through it was in summer no more than two or there feet deep. In winter it was a roaring torrent. Down in the Cut were some of the finest trout I have ever seen. I fish for them now in imagination. I like to think they have eluded others and have preserved themselves. The Cut was full of insect and vegetable life, so that these trout disdained all lures on hooks. The blackthorn, elders and hawthorns that overhung the sides of the Cut and made an impenetrable wall for the safety of cattle and small boys gave shade and cool mooring to these trout. When they tired of the shade they would come out to the middle of the stream and hover there, ignoring the morsels of food that drifted past them, just as they ignored the bait I sometimes dangled from the bridge. If I threw a pebble they would be gone, swiftly, like the blink of an eye. In a little while one would come backing downstream and another up the water to take up position there in the middle where the current had some special sweetness or warmth. In half an hour ten or a dozen would be hovering in the centre below the arch of the bridge.

Visitors who came suggested all sorts of ways of catching these fine fish, but no one I knew of ever managed the feat. They may hover there today in the sunlight with the endless passage of the white clouds high above them.

One summer the Cut gave protection to a mallard and her brood of young. They paddled in echelon upstream. When the mother saw me she took flight and her yellow and brown mottled family hastily went into the shelter of the stone slabs, vanishing as completely as the trout sometimes did.

The Modern Market

WHILE we still talk of the ways of fish, of poaching trout and salmon, and in case you choose to make a living in such a risky fashion, let me say something about the market. There is a market in salmon, legal or illegal. Trout can always be sold at a fair enough price, but salmon is a matter controlled by the bigger business. There was a time when the poacher worked on his own, secured his market, filled his orders, setting about the actual business of getting his fish after he knew, more or less, who would take them, and, in fact, destroying or burying the excess to keep the price up when need be. It was a shameful thing to hawk fish and a dangerous thing too. Today things are a little different. The merchants have deep-freeze units. Salmon can be accommodated whenever they are available, the quantity having only a small effect on the price. Salmon isn't out of season when the waiter takes the order nowadays. A glut in October can be evened out in the months of the close season, hence the arduous work of the gangs who operate without scruple and come back to the pools again and again. The penalties are not what they were, of course. The rewards are greater and the punishment fits the crime, at least in Scotland where the salmon is a national industry and a tourist attraction.

Could it be said that poaching a river, a stream or a lake is a greater crime than poaching a fallow of its partridges, a covert of its pheasants, a hill of the hare? I think it depends on how a man feels about fish and rivers, game and the woods and moors. It is a great deal easier for the scoundrel to ruin a river and its stock of fish than it used to be. The remote places of my childhood are remote no more. There are wild moors where the black cock crows, where the stag stands surveying the morning and an eagle sails above the mountain crags beyond, but rivers are less remote because roads run beside them, because transport has opened the way to the far Cuilins and streams that flow to the sea in countless gorges where the salmon ascend. It cannot be said that the salmon belongs only to the rich man who was once bothered by poachers as he might have been bothered by a rain fly as he inspected his preserves in midsummer. Salmon fishing, fishing of any sort, is the pastime, relaxation and delight of countless thousands who love to get away from their fellows and stand not in the roar of the city but the sound of murmuring waters. The man who plunders paradise with explosives, net and spear is beyond the pale. The magistrates were not always hard on the old poacher, the character whose plea was plausible and whose manner ingratiating. Not a few had compassion on him, for they knew temptation themselves. Indeed, one or two magistrates and civic dignitaries in my part of the world have themselves fallen by the wayside of late. Altogether it is fitting that the poaching of water is a more heinous crime in the eyes of authority.

Of poaching as a whole I might speak a final warning. The risks are great and the penalties are heavy. It is perhaps as well to sleep soundly at nights and leave such adventures to desperate characters like Snib. The habit, once it takes, grows and absorbs a man's thoughts. Every time he finds himself in a quiet village with a stream he begins to study the water and wonder whether there are fish to be had, and his conscience about licence or ownership of water fades and vanishes like the froth churned among the stones. A man cannot be really virtuous until he has known temptation. The temptation is an old one and one which can be stirred in the most self-respecting.

I have lately taken to staying at home. Sometimes the curlews call as they fly over at night and I think of the journeys I made across the moss. Sometimes I get a vision of a boulder-strewn river coming through a wooded valley and I feel restless. The pigeons call from the woodside on a misty autumn evening; I walk up through the hills and hear the partridge calling the covey together or the rasping note of the cock pheasant, and I curse my newly-found respectability. I think of Jeck and his kind. I dream and catch my first hare again. I know that in the farmland behind the village a boy from a cottage is setting his first snare or studying the movement of the birds. I can be for ever young. Perhaps the thing with poachers is that they never grow old, at least in this one respect that they have the energy for the meandering journey to the back of beyond, the patience to shelter for two or three hours in the fringe of the wood, the capacity to become absorbed in hunting and to study all the ways of nature.

There are vagabonds among them and desperate and shiftless characters. Forget the lessons of Francie, Little Hugh, Black Bill and the rest, and let the night be a time for going to a comfortable bed.

I hope I have not disturbed you, but if ever you want to buy an old gun, a ferret, or even a well-trained dog . . .